Compacts and Smoking Accessories

Roseann Ettinger

Schiffer Publishing Ltd

1469 Morstein Road, West Chester, Pennsylvania 19380

Dedication

To My Parents,
Vito and Marie Rodino,
With Love.

Acknowledgements

I would like to thank my brother and his wife, John and Ester Rodino, and my sister and her husband, Veeta Marie and Joseph Polchin, for their sincere efforts in encouraging me through this endeavor. Thank you again, Mom, Dad, Terry, Clint and Amber for your support.

My sincere appreciation to the following people who graciously allowed me to photograph some wonderful examples found throughout this book: Christine Ketchel; Ann Marsh; John Morse Jr.; Marceline Lotman and George Wurtzel (Her Own Place).

Special thanks to Ceil Lee for making one dream come true; and to the great staff of the Big Picture Company, Mt. Laurel, New Jersey.

Three piece set consisting of oval compact, perfume vial and cigarette lighter decorated with enamel and hand painted flowers, marked Evans.

Copyright © 1991 by Roseann Ettinger.
Library of Congress Catalog Number: 91-65660.

Printed in the United States of America.
ISBN: 0-88740-371-9

Published by Schiffer Publishing, Ltd.
1469 Morstein Road
West Chester, Pennsylvania 19380
Please write for a free catalog.
This book may be purchased from the publisher.
Please include $2.00 postage.
Try your bookstore first.

We are interested in hearing from authors with book ideas on related subjects.

Preface

In the late nineteenth century, enormous attitude changes occurred with respect to women wearing makeup. By the early twentieth century, it was no longer viewed as vulgar or immoral and as a result, it began to appear as a normal practice. With this new standard and the growing demand for cosmetics, manufacturers were prompted to produce receptacles specifically designed for holding these cosmetic preparations. These receptacles were sometimes attached to short chains and carried instead of a handbag; they were called vanity cases. Often they were fitted with extra compartments for holding coins, calling cards and possibly handkerchiefs. Smaller containers were manufactured for holding only face powder or rouge and were usually carried inside of a handbag; these cases were called compacts. By the 1920s, these popular accessories were cleverly designed to hold cigarettes as well.

The male practice of smoking cigarettes began to catch on in the United States following the Civil War. The process of blending different tobacco leaves led to a dramatic increase in consumption around 1900. By World War I, smoking taboos were finally lifted for women so that they could enjoy smoking in public. This increased use of tobacco contributed to the development of match safes, lighters, cigar and cigarette cases.

Compacts and Smoking Accessories was written to present a brief history of cosmetics and the early vanity cases and compacts designed to carry cosmetic applications; it was also written to present a brief history of tobacco and its historical significance leading to the manufacture of popular smoking accessories used by both men and women.

Collecting vanity cases, compacts and smoking accessories has become a very widespread hobby enjoyed by men and women alike. Because of this relatively new field of collecting, more information is required. These fashion accessories were extremely popular throughout the first half of the twentieth century and there were so many manufacturers that it is impossible to include them all in one volume. The most popular vanity case and compact manufacturers are highlighted in addition to the popular cigarette case and lighter manufacturers. So much more is still waiting to be uncovered in this exciting field.

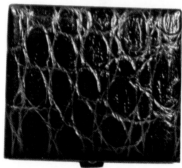

Snakeskin and alligator compacts marked "A Dorette Creation."

Values

To place a value on a vanity case, compact or smoking accessory, many factors are taken into consideration. First of all, the material with which a particular accessory is made is very important: precious metals such as solid gold, platinum and sterling silver are much more valuable than gold-, silver-, chromium-, rhodium- or nickel-plated examples. If an accessory is set with stones, careful scrutiny must reveal whether the stones are gems, synthetics, pastes, brilliants, rhinestones or glass. Materials that resemble natural ivory, amber and tortoiseshell should be tested to determine their authenticity; celluloid, Bakelite and a host of other plastics are made to resemble natural materials. Hand-made versus machine-made technique, rarity of a design, country of origin and identifying marks leading to the date of manufacture are all important. Patent numbers are frequently found on these accessories which accurately date a particular piece. Condition, original presentation box, original fittings, stature of the manufacturer, designed by someone famous, and the never-ending law of supply and demand are all important factors in determining value.

Vanity cases, compacts and smoking accessories previously owned by famous people bring extremely high prices on today's market, especially at recent auctions. Sadly, extremely high prices have been paid for these little gems with less attention to the composition of a piece. For example, a sterling silver cigarette case once belonging to Rita Hayworth sold for over $5000. Because of these factors, collecting compacts and smoking accessories is beginning to be taken very seriously.

Prices also vary dramatically from one locale to another. Therefore, a value guide, rather than a specific price guide, will be included in the back of the book.

Goldtone carryall with popular basket-weave design, accented with rhinestones and mesh strap handle.

Ornate heart-shaped compact made of brass accented with scrolling designs and genuine stones, Middle Eastern influence.

Contents

Title page photos:
Left—Match safe made of nickel plate over brass with embossed design of a deer on one side and a floral border on the opposite side, Pat. Jan. 12, 1904.
Center—Ornate match safe with embossed designs, marked Silveroin.
Right—Round compact made of gold electroplate and enamel and accented with smooth and faceted imitation stones, marked Paris Presents Ltd., Made in Great Britian.

Tango chain double vanity made of chromium plate and red enamel, marked Vashé.

Goldtone cigarette case decorated with imitation stones.

Chapter I: Brief History of Cosmetics

While cosmetics were present in many ancient civilizations, either for the purpose of personal adornment or for use in a specific tribal ritual, it was not until the late nineteenth century that manufacturers began to produce face powders and rouge in great numbers.

Egypt

The ancient Egyptians used a significant amount of eyepaint for shaping the eyebrows and eyelids as well as for protection from the sun. Black antimony powder, galena and kohl were used. During the Middle Ages, reddish rouge, made of mercury and sulphur compounds, and white face powder, made of lead compounds, were the predominant substances used to paint the face. The chosen colors of red (rouge) and white (powder) were to remind one of the rose and the lily, the "flowers of romantic chivalry." Protection from the sun was also a prime reason for the use of white face powder and the rouge was to achieve a youthful appearance.

Renaissance

During the Renaissance, a time of rebirth which marked the end of the Middle Ages, attitudes changed in Europe. Italy, well ahead of the other countries in intellectual and artistic expression, took the lead in cosmetic preparation and application. Italian women wore a tremendous amount of face makeup with French women following close behind. Due to a more Puritan way of life, Englishwomen were slower to catch on to this practice. When Elizabeth I ascended the throne in 1558 however, a dramatic metamorphosis occurred in England. Not long after Elizabeth's coronation, cosmetic preparation and application became common practice. Elizabeth was self-conscious of the image she portrayed. She possessed a burning desire to preserve her beauty. Having been a fashion dictator, cosmetic application followed suit. Elizabeth, as well as the ladies of her court, wore plenty of white face powder, cheek rouge and lip dye. Constantly

Opposite page:
Harrison Fisher, circa 1910.

The Name
Freeman
On
Face
Powder
Means
Highest Quality
Freeman Perfume Company, Cincinnati, Ohio

Freeman Face Powder advertisement featured in the *Ladies' Home Journal*, circa 1912.

LADIES ATTENTION
The Princess Beautifier is ..... or to all face powders. Removes all blemishes of the skin ..... as Freckles, Pimples and Wrinkles, prevents Tan and Chapping Price 50 cents. Free samples.
THE PRINCESS TOILET CO., LOS ANGELES

Advertisement for The Princess Beautifier Face Powder, circa 1912.

Edwardian woman holding elegant hand mirror. *Delineator*, 1902.

gazing into their looking glasses, Elizabethan women became obsessed with their beauty. Ironically, this obsession to preserve their youth and beauty through makeup aided in the deterioration of their skin due to the toxicity of the applied substances.

Seventeenth Century

By the seventeenth century, men as well as women wore face makeup. Again, abundant use of white lead face powder, rouge and lip dye was common practice. Men and women both curled and powdered their hair, and wigs were often worn. Since bathing was paradoxically an uncommon practice at the time, the powder and the wigs were used primarily to camouflage the unclean hair underneath. These toxic substances which were supposed to enhance beauty, continued to work in the opposite direction.

This obsession led to a continual search for products to improve the complexion and enhance one's beauty. Housewives began making homemade preparations while alchemists and charlatans continually allured the unsuspecting society belle with magical creams and lotions. The preparations were very expensive and most proved worthless in the final analysis. Nevertheless, the vanity continued and the search went on for the fountain of youth.

Eighteenth Century

In the eighteenth century, white lead was still used as the main component for face plasterings. How incredible it was that men and women were so ignorant of its toxic properties! But the vanity continued to obstruct clear thought and basic common sense. Extravagant use of cosmetics led to the elaborate containers designed to hold them. Boudoir dressing tables were full of powder jars, puffs, rouge pots and scent bottles.

In the early part of the eighteenth century, a tremendous amount of one's day was spent preparing the body with various cosmetic applications. By the close of the same century, however, these vain practices were becoming vulgar and immoral. The French Revolution in 1789 had a great deal to do with the lessening desire for cosmetics.

Mennen's Face Powder advertisement, circa 1912.

Freeman's Face Powder advertisement, January, 1912.

Nineteenth Century

By the nineteenth century, cosmetics were again popularized, but they were now made with natural ingredients instead of with toxic white lead. Homemade preparations were preferred over store bought substances. Talc was now the main ingredient in face powder and the dyes for rouge were vegetable in origin. Cosmetics were again essential and women used them in excess once more. In 1806, a French fashion journal commented that ladies' rouge containers were an essential part of their cosmetic *toilette*. At the same time, Napoleon's wife, Josephine was said to have spent more than three thousand francs a year on rouge. Since Josephine was another fashion dictator, the public, imitating her style, followed suit.

In the 1820s and 1830s, rouge was still in vogue. In the next decade, however, its popularity diminished as the young Queen Victoria ascended the throne in England in 1837. At that time, cosmetics were applied sparingly. Women's fashion publications were continually trying to inform and educate the public on the use of homemade preparations made of natural ingredients. Cleanliness was now stressed more than ever before. Men and women of the previous centuries had basically been ignorant of the fact that soap and water could achieve marvelous results in cleansing their complexions not to mention eliminating body odors. Instead of bathing, however, they chose to cover and mask their smells and imperfections with scents, facial paints and powders. In England, now under the rule of Victoria, this changed as cleanliness became a virtue and bathing became common practice. The soap industry flourished.

With strict moral attitudes, many frowned upon women of decency wearing makeup. By 1850, slightly rouge-colored cheeks and pearl face powder were used "discreetly" by women in Europe. It was not until the Civil War that American women began to wear face makeup, and only in a conservative manner. By the early 1860s, dyeing the hair and wearing heavy face makeup was again fashionable. By 1868, women were wearing wigs and painting their eyes as well. It became, as one nineteenth century essayist called it, "...national madness" and people of strict moral backgrounds waited patiently until the madness again passed.

In England, by the late 1800s, Victorian attitudes still frowned upon the use of cosmetics. Theatrical women and harlots wore makeup to paint their faces. Everyone else was expected to rely on nature, proper diet and exercise to achieve those rosy cheeks, lily face and ruby lips. Fashion magazines continually printed articles for women to inform them of the various methods of achieving that healthy glow without the use of face plasterings. Those who chose to wear cosmetics did so in secrecy. By the

Pears' Soap, September, 1912.

Opposite page:
Mavis Face Powder advertisement featured in *Pictorial Review*, March, 1922.

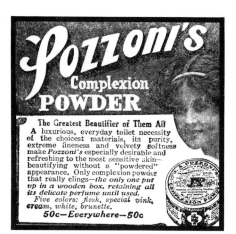

Pozzoni's Complexion Powder advertisement, February 15, 1912.

Mary Garden Double Compact designed to hold powder and rouge, circa 1926.

Gay Nineties', attitudes began to lighten as a direct result of women's emancipation. This liberation accounted for an entirely new outlook towards femininity. Actresses of the theatre, like Sarah Bernhardt, wore makeup both on and off the stage. Society belle, Lily Langtry, was seen in "discreet" cosmetic ads for the popular Pears' Soap. The secrecy of buying and wearing cosmetics was finally coming to an end.

Twentieth Century

When Victoria's reign was ended by her death in 1901, and the Edwardian era began, a more relaxed atmosphere allowed women to liberally apply their cosmetics without fear of criticism. Queen Alexandra, who had been a fashion dictator even before her reign, wore cosmetics, and women tried to emulate her good looks by wearing makeup also. Fewer preparations were made at home. Since respectable women were now using cosmetics, the manufactured preparations were acceptable and preferred.

In the 1890s, Helena Rubinstein became an innovator in the field of cosmetics. She introduced a line of face powder that was tinted to resemble natural skin tones instead of the stark white color that was previously used. She also introduced eye shadows and mascara. Makeup was becoming widely accepted in England, America and Australia. By 1902, she opened a salon in Melbourne and, after much success there, she opened a salon in London, Paris and New York. By 1918, Helena Rubinstein had salons in Chicago, Philadelphia, New Orleans, San Francisco and Atlantic City.

Another famous beauty expert who revolutionized the cosmetic industry was Elizabeth Arden. Born Florence Nightingale Graham on New Year's Eve in 1878, Elizabeth Arden opened her first salon in 1910. Her philosophy and attitude toward cosmetics focused on a concept known as "total skin care." With a nursing and pharmaceutical background, her theories were taken very seriously and she became highly acclaimed worldwide.

In the first decade of the twentieth century, mail-order catalogues offered many imported face powders made of the "very finest sifted rice flour and delightfully perfumed." Each brand was advertised as "free from any harmful ingredients" or "injurious substances." They were available in three shades: white, flesh and brunette. Other cosmetic companies began to manufacture face powder which "blended softly and invisibly...without the questionable suggestion of makeup." This popular brand of powder was called *Jonteel. Mary Garden Face Powder and Rouge* by Rigaud of Paris was also advertised tremendously in the early twentieth century. Its claim to fame was that it "blended with your coloring." *Lablanche Face Powder* was quite popular in the early teens. Perfect beauty was stressed by

Jonteel Face Powder and Rouge, circa 1920.

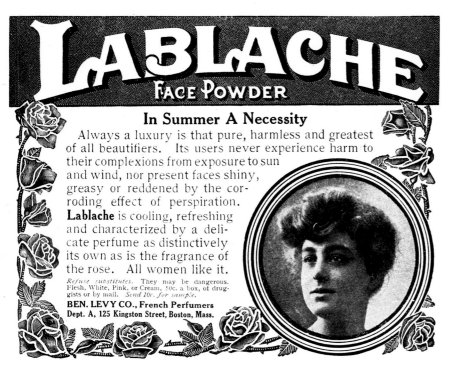

In Summer A Necessity

Always a luxury is that pure, harmless and greatest of all beautifiers. Its users never experience harm to their complexions from exposure to sun and wind, nor present faces shiny, greasy or reddened by the corroding effect of perspiration. **Lablache** is cooling, refreshing and characterized by a delicate perfume as distinctively its own as is the fragrance of the rose. All women like it.

Refuse substitutes. They may be dangerous. Flesh, White, Pink, or Cream, 50c. a box, of druggists or by mail. *Send 10c. for sample.*

BEN. LEVY CO., French Perfumers
Dept. A, 125 Kingston Street, Boston, Mass.

Lablanche Face Powder advertisement, July, 1909.

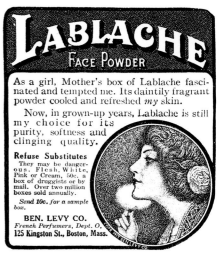

As a girl, Mother's box of Lablache fascinated and tempted me. Its daintily fragrant powder cooled and refreshed *my* skin.

Now, in grown-up years, Lablache is still my choice for its purity, softness and clinging quality.

Refuse Substitutes
They may be dangerous. Flesh, White, Pink or Cream, 50c. a box of druggists or by mail. Over two million boxes sold annually.
Send 10c. for a sample box.

BEN. LEVY CO.
French Perfumers, Dept. O,
125 Kingston St., Boston, Mass.

Lablanche Face Powder advertisement, November, 1922.

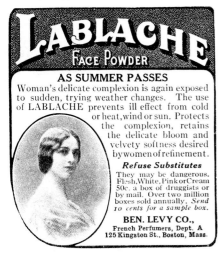

AS SUMMER PASSES

Woman's delicate complexion is again exposed to sudden, trying weather changes. The use of LABLACHE prevents ill effect from cold or heat, wind or sun. Protects the complexion, retains the delicate bloom and velvety softness desired by women of refinement.

Refuse Substitutes
They may be dangerous. Flesh, White, Pink or Cream 50c. a box of druggists or by mail. Over two million boxes sold annually. *Send 10 cents for a sample box.*

BEN. LEVY CO.,
French Perfumers, Dept. A
125 Kingston St., Boston, Mass.

Lablanche Face Powder advertisement, circa 1912.

THE RETURN TO OUTDOORS

marks a trying time for dainty complexions and tender skins. LABLACHE, the powder invisible, protects and perpetuates that velvety smoothness. Used by millions of discriminating women the world over. Exquisitely fragrant. A constant delight.

Refuse Substitutes
They may be dangerous. Flesh, White, Pink or Cream, 50c. a box of druggists or by mail. Over two million boxes sold annually. *Send 10c. for a sample box.*

BEN. LEVY CO.
French Perfumers, Dept. 49
125 Kingston St., Boston, Mass.

Lablanche Face Powder advertisement, May, 1914.

this company stating that: "Thousands of women gain that confidence by using *Lablanche*. It beautifies the delicate skin tissues, smoothes the wrinkles and gives the skin that youthful velvety appearance which impacts the desirable touch of refinement." Every ad contained a warning to "refuse substitutes, they may be dangerous." It finally became apparent that previous preparations were harmful.

The outbreak of World War I caused an increase in the number of women joining the work force. Women now had lives outside of their homes and they wanted to look fashionable, professional or just feel feminine. All of these factors had a direct result on the use of cosmetics. The cosmetic industry became a big money-making enterprise with advertising campaigns everywhere. Liberation allowed women to wear makeup without any stigma attached whatsoever.

Although some type of lip tint, dye or paste had been around for centuries, the actual metal lipstick tube was not introduced until around 1915. Lipstick became the rage in the Roaring Twenties when the flapper tried to shock the world with her vampish looks. The bobbed hair, the dark and harsh penciled eyebrows and the scarlet lips were a definite jolt after the very feminine Gibson Girl of a few years earlier.

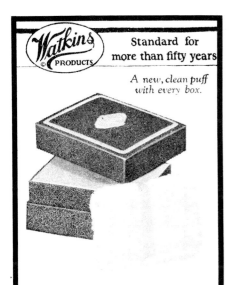
Watkins Garda Face Powder, November, 1922.

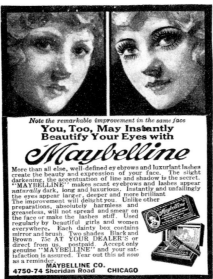
Maybelline advertisement featured in *Pictorial Review*, November, 1922.

Circa 1925.

Advertisement for Max Factor "Color Harmony" make-up, *Ladies' Home Journal*, June, 1944.

Advertisement for Max Factor make-up, *McCall's*, March, 1938.

"Harmonizing" cosmetics by Richard Hudnut, circa 1936.

And HE will tell you, "You're gorgeous tonight!"

IT'S NEW ... it's different ... it's excitingly better . . . Marvelous the Matched Makeup, by Richard Hudnut.

For here at last is makeup that ends clashing colors . . . a makeup that matches . . . face powder, rouge, lipstick, eye shadow, and mascara, all in scientific color symphony.

And—more important—here's makeup that you can easily choose in the certainty that it matches *you!* For it is keyed to your own personality color, the color that never changes, *the color of your eyes.*

Discover Marvelous the new Eye-Matched Makeup. Eight out of ten girls who try it are lovelier, *immediately* more glamorous.

At your drug or department store now . . . guaranteed for purity by the world-famous house of Richard Hudnut ... full-size packages ... 55 cents each. Ask for Marvelous Dresden type face powder, rouge, lipstick, eye shadow and mascara if your eyes are blue; Parisian if your eyes are brown; Patrician if they are gray; Continental if they are hazel.

Wear Marvelous the Eye-Matched Makeup and hear the man you like best exclaim: "You're *gorgeous* tonight!"

COPR. 1936. RICHARD HUDNUT

SPECIAL! Your local drug and department stores are featuring at 55¢ a $1.00-value Marvelous Matched Makeup Kit—containing junior sizes of harmonizing face powder, rouge, lipstick, mascara, and eye shadow ... keyed to the color of your eyes. Or send 55¢ direct to Richard Hudnut, 5th Ave., New York, stating whether your eyes are blue, gray, brown, or hazel, and we'll mail kit.

55¢ *each*

MARVELOUS *The Eye-Matched* MAKEUP
by RICHARD HUDNUT

Cosmetics by Richard Hudnut advertised in *Pictorial Review*, May, 1936.

By the 1930s, the stars of the screen constantly appeared wearing makeup on and off the screen. Fashion publications were filled with cosmetic ads with actresses promoting specific products. Max Factor of Hollywood continually marketed their products throughout this decade by using prominent celebrities to promote their face makeup. Stars like Franciska Gaal, Tala Birell, Florence Rice, Barbara Stanwyck, Marion Marsh and Claudette Colbert were seen throughout the thirties in ads for Max Factor "color harmony" makeup.

Beauty preparations by Richard Hudnut were also quite common at that time. The color harmony concept, using makeup that "matched" rather than "clashed", was the philosophy behind the company's marketing strategy. They stressed that you "choose your makeup by the color of your eyes!" If this is done, you become "immediately more glamourous." That was the key word and every woman strived to achieve that glamourous Hollywood look.

Powder and rouge containers by DuBarry and Heather Theatrical Rouge.

Four early powder compact refills in original boxes by Houbigant, Richard Hudnut, Coty and Harriet Hubbard Ayer.

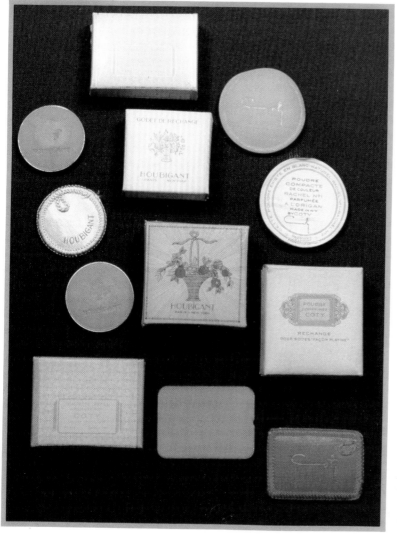

Houbigant and Coty powder and rouge refills.

Cosmetics by Louis Philippe popular in 1936.

A 1943 advertisement for Flame-Glo cosmetics with new packaging due to war restrictions.

LIPSTICK

Only a marvelously smooth-spreading Lipstick... in true Youth-Tone tints... can supply this delicate, 'teen-age coloring! The flattering color becomes indelible, by the simple trick of moistening your lips before you apply it. Three shades. A stunning, modern case.

Seventeen Lipstick and Rouge advertised in *McCall's* magazine in April, 1932.

ROUGE

Use Seventeen Rouge with Seventeen Lipstick, to create perfect, natural coloring! The color tints of Seventeen Rouge are based on the ACTUAL COLORING OF YOUTHFUL SKIN; so, if you use your proper shade, the effect will be natural and charming always. Five Youth-Tone shades.

POWDER

Try Seventeen Two-Tone Powder, and you will say it's the most exciting powder discovery you ever made! The Two-Tone effect is produced by blending two weights of powder. The heavier clings closely to the skin, seems slightly darker. The lighter weight powder, on the surface, creates a subtle overtone, which lends an appearance of youthful, delicate transparency. What a glorious difference from the masking dullness of ordinary powders!

Seventeen Face Powder advertised in *McCall's* magazine in April, 1932.

Poudre Incarnat by Louis Philippe, the French colorist, also created a sensation in the 1930s. Again, the color harmony concept was used as the face powder coordinated with the lipstick. The same harmony was expected when the rouge and lipstick were worn together. Specific coordinating shades were designed for blondes, brunettes and redheads.

Coty's *Air Spun* face powder was advertised as "the revolutionary new face powder" because it combined various shades of powder with different perfume scents "spun together in a whirling, swirling cyclone of air!" Other popular face powders of the period were Azurea, Carmen, Djer-Kiss, Jaccard, LeTrefle, Mavis, Melba, Nadine, Pompeian and Woodbury.

Many cosmetic companies stressed a "softer" look. Powder was now offered in a large variety of shades that were very close to natural skin tones. Powders were designed to create illusions of younger looking skin and cosmetic companies used these gimmicks to increase their sales. Fashion magazines provided tips on the proper methods of applying makeup. Each season offered cosmetic lines with many new harmonious shades to choose from. The buying public was overwhelmed with the choices of colors that were available for face powders, rouges and lipsticks. Cosmetics were here to stay.

Maddening Hues

FOR LIPS AND CHEEKS

A NEW KIND OF LIPSTICK...A NEW KIND OF DRY ROUGE WORK MIRACLES IN RED

Maddening hues, yes! Colors that thrill, taunt and tempt! Truly enough (*and you'll know it the instant you try them*) such rapturous, wicked reds have never been used in lipstick or rouge before. But there's more reason than that for the soul-stirring madness so generously imparted by SAVAGE Lipstick and the new SAVAGE Rouge.

SAVAGE Lipstick works differently from ordinary lipstick. Its gorgeous color separates from the cosmetic after application to become an actual part of the skin. Wipe the cosmetic away and see your lips teasingly, savagely red . . . but without the usual discouraging pastiness. Imagine a lipstick like that! Better yet, experience its magic on your own lips. One or more of the four luscious SAVAGE shades is sure to be exactly yours.

SAVAGE Rouge . . . an utterly new kind of dry rouge . . . so much finer in texture than any other that it blends right into the skin itself . . . to stay, with full color intensity, throughout the exciting hours it invites, instead of quickly fading away as ordinary rouge does. You'll love it, and the shades are identical to those of SAVAGE Lipstick so that your cheeks and lips will be a thrilling, perfect symphony of maddening, meaningful red.

Then . . . SAVAGE Face Powder

And what a different face powder *this* is; so fine, soft, smooth and so surprisingly different in the results it gives. Apply it, and it seems to vanish . . . but the skin-shine, too, has gone. Imagine it! Everything you want from powder, but no "powdered" look; just caressing soft smoothness that is a feast for eyes and a tingle for finger tips it makes so eager. Four lovely shades.

20¢ AT ALL TEN CENT STORES

TANGERINE • FLAME
NATURAL • BLUSH

Savage Cream
Rouge . . . for
lips and cheeks

NATURAL
(Flesh)
BEIGE
RACHEL
RACHEL
(Extra Dark)

"Savage" brand cosmetics popular in 1935.

Elegant brass vanity case suspended from chain enriched with imitation stones and pearls, large tassel and silk lined interior.

Chapter II: Vanity Cases and Compacts

The importance of the purse over the centuries has remained an obvious formality. Chosen items of necessity for men and women were carried conveniently in various shaped receptacles. Initially, these receptacles were solely utilitarian but they evolved into ornamental appendages throughout certain periods. One particular item that women carried in their purse or by itself for over a half a century was the vanity case or compact to hold cosmetics.

With the growing popularity for cosmetics in the late nineteenth century, and as the cosmetic industry blossomed into a huge industry, containers to hold these cosmetics became just as necessary. To house such preparations for personal adornment, the vanity case became extremely fashionable. Vanity cases were so-named because of the stigma that had been attached to wearing makeup. Plastering powder and rouge on one's face was still not a totally accepted behavior. Women's emancipation, however, allowed the stigma to wear off and the makeup to go on!

Gilded brass vanity case accented with bezel-set imitation stones.

Vanity purse with 50-inch chain, circa 1900

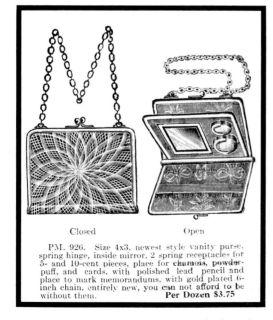

PM. 926. Size 4x3, newest style vanity purse, spring hinge, inside mirror, 2 spring receptacles for 5- and 10-cent pieces, place for chamois, powder-puff, and cards, with polished lead pencil and place to mark memorandums, with gold plated 6-inch chain, entirely new, you can not afford to be without them. **Per Dozen $3.75**

Vanity case shown open and closed, M. Gerber, circa 1900.

Vanity case made of sterling silver with repoussé work. This vanity case was originally part of a chatelaine. *John Morse Jr..*

German silver vanity case with engraved top, inside fitted with two coin holders, card or money holder and powder compact.

Brass vanity case with heavy embossed designs, paste stone set in center, inside fitted with coin holder, powder compartment, mirror and calling card holder.

Vanity Cases

The vanity case was very much a part of the fashion scene in the early twentieth century. Vanities were designed in all shapes and sizes with compartments for coins and calling cards in conjunction with "toilet requisites" such as powder, rouge and lipstick. The powder was primarily the loose powder beneath a sifter of one form or another. The inside was fitted with a glass mirror or a piece of polished steel which served as a mirror. The internal fittings were basically standard although the layout varied from one vanity case to another. Octagonal-shaped vanity cases were often suspended from four-inch chains with an attached finger ring for carrying. This type of case was sometimes referred to as a "Dorine Case." The Dorine case could be made of solid gold, yellow or white gold-filled, sterling silver, plated base metals, aluminum, brass, gunmetal and gilt. It came fitted with a powder puff and mirror. Rectangular vanity cases, attached to short metal chains or finger rings, were extremely fashionable as well.

Sterling silver vanity purse with chain handle, hand engraved, monogrammed and marked Sterling, Blackinton Mfg. Co., circa 1900. *Her Own Place.*

German silver vanity case (chain is missing).

Inside view of German silver vanity case revealing mirror, large leather pocket, powder compartment and three coin holders.

Embossed vanity case made of silver-plated metal, fitted with compartments for powder, rouge and lipstick, marked Elgin Clock Co., E A M.

Engraved vanity case with shield for
monogram, marked German Silver.

Inside view of German silver vanity
case revealing mirror, two coin holders,
powder compartment and space for
paper money or calling cards.

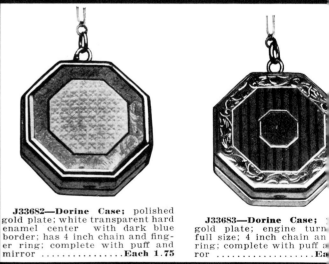

J33682—Dorine Case; polished
gold plate; white transparent hard
enamel center with dark blue
border; has 4 inch chain and finger ring; complete with puff and
mirror ....Each 1.75

J33683—Dorine Case;
gold plate; engine turn
full size; 4 inch chain an
ring; complete with puff a
ror ....Ea

Dorine cases offered for sale in 1920.

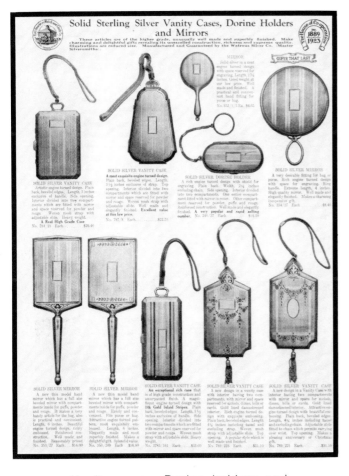

Vanity cases, Dorine holders and mirrors made of sterling silver popular in 1923.

White metal enameled compacts and vanity case chains featured in the Benj. Allen & Co. wholesale catalogue, circa 1935.

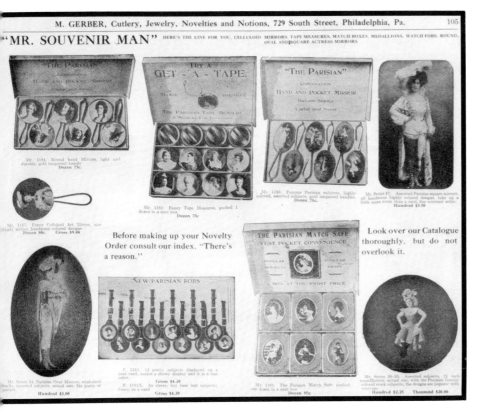

Celluloid novelties popular around 1900.

Exquisitely crafted gilded brass, ormolu (gilded bronze), vermeil or gilded base metal vanities were produced in Austria, France, England and Italy around the turn of the century. These cases were frequently designed in openwork or filigree patterns accented with exquisite enamel work and enriched with gemstones. Early plastics, such as celluloid and Bakelite, were also used in abundance and quite often garnished with imitation stones. These cases were popular in the late teens and early twenties. The French created elaborate examples of Bakelite cases in a wide array of colors with paste ornamentation, silk cords and tassels.

Vanity cases made of base metals were often plated with chromium and later rhodium to prevent tarnishing. Both chromium and rhodium belong to the platinum family so the expensive look prevailed. Engine-turned designs were applied for embellishment along with delicate enamel work. Chromium-plated vanity cases and compacts made by Coty were often referred to as "Platinum-Toned."

Vanity case made of gilded brass suspended from chain handle.

Inside view of gilded brass vanity case.

Two gilded brass vanity cases with ornate openwork designs further embellished with imitation stones and pearls. The case on the right is marked "Trinity Plate."

Round vanity case suspended from chain made of chromium plate with enameled front, hand engraving and engine-turned designs. The inside is fitted with compartments for powder, rouge, lipstick and solid perfume, unmarked. Gold plated vanity case, hand engraved, marked Coro.

Two chromium-plated vanity cases with enamel ornamentation, hand painted flowers and engine-turned designs. The case on the left was patented on February 9, 1926.

Oblong vanity case with chain handle made of 14K gold embellished with diamonds and sapphires. The inside is fitted with powder and rouge compartments, circa 1930. *Her Own Place.*

Combination hand mirror with compact made of a silvered base metal and embossed designs. This was a souvenir of Bushkill Falls, Pennsylvania.

Star-shaped vanity case with attached chain handle made of chromium plate and an enamel medallion mounted in the center. *John Morse Jr..*

In January, 1905, *The Designer Magazine* commented on vanity cases:

"For the woman who is always careful of her personal appearance there is a wonderfully attractive toilet and card case combined. Suspended from her wrist by a chain and containing separate compartments for a powder-puff, beauty plasters, mirror, visiting cards and small change, the society belle carries her vanity case all day long. Very elaborate are some of these little cases made of gold and having pearls set in the back, or perhaps the monogram done in colored stones. Silver is not so popular as at one time when purses, belts, chatelaines and back combs of the metal were displayed on all sides. Those having handsome silver jewelry have sent them to be gilded."

By the end of the first decade of the twentieth century, silver was again fashionable in addition to the increasing use of platinum.

Vanity cases, obviously, were treated with much the same respect as jewelry and other decorative arts. They displayed specific characteristics of each particular period in which they were made. For example, in the late nineteenth century, extremely ornate, sometimes ostentatious vanity cases were made which incorporated filigree, tassels, gemstones, heavy engraving and repoussé work which reflected the essence of the Victorian style. Vanity cases made during the Art Nouveau period displayed free-flowing lines and a sinuous style reminiscent of the Arts and Crafts style from the 1890s to the onset of the first world war. At the turn of the century, vanity cases were designed with the flamboyant richness of the opulent Edwardian era depicting garland and laurel wreath motifs, *guilloché* enameling and engine-turned engraving. The compacts and vanity cases of the Art Deco period were rich in bright colored enamel in geometric patterns reflecting the look of a modern era.

This sterling silver vanity case with hammered designs was offered for $37.00 in 1920.

This engraved vanity case made of sterling silver was offered for $30.00 in 1920.

Woman holding vanity case, *The Designer*, November, 1923.

Oval double vanity case with engine-turned designs and cloisonné medallion, marked S.O.B.

Left—Vanity case, nickel-plated over brass, fitted with compartments for powder, rouge, calling cards or paper money. Right—Silver-plated vanity case with engraved and embossed designs fitted with coin holders, powder and money compartments and mirror.

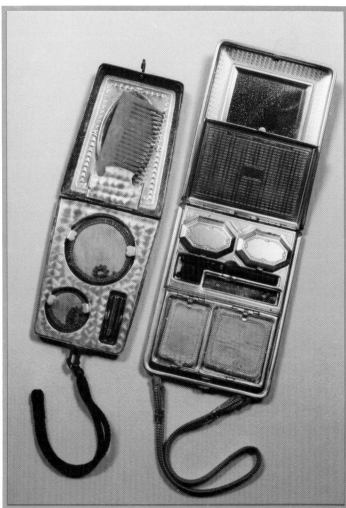

Left—Nickel silver vanity case fitted with mirror, celluloid comb, powder and rouge compartment and small lip paste tube, marked Evans. Right—Vanity case fitted with mirror and compartments for powder, rouge, lip paste, eye shadow and mascara, marked Mondaine, NY, USA.

Finger ring vanity case, rhodium-plated ith engine-turned designs and black enamel ornamentation.

Triple vanity case accented with bright enamel ornamentation in geometric zig zag designs suspended from chain, marked Elgin American.

Modernistic vanity case made of goldtone metal, black and green striped enamel and black Bakelite suspended from black grosgrain wrist cord with two brass adjustable sliders. The inside is fitted with powder, rouge and lipstick compartments, coin holder, mirror and money clip, marked Terri Vanity, 4 W. 40th Street, New York, NY.

Two black enameled vanity cases with wrist cords by "Terri." The inside of each vanity case is fitted with two rectangular compartments for powder and rouge, a small round well for lip paste, a coin holder, mirror and clip for holding paper money.

Because trends and influences continually overlapped from one period to the next, elaborately engraved Victorian and Edwardian-style compacts and vanity cases were still manufactured into the 1920s. In 1923, a wholesale house known as The Fort Dearborn Watch and Clock Company offered a large selection of sterling silver and silver-plated vanity cases fitted with powder puffs, mirrors, coin and card holders. These thin-modeled cases were engraved with engine-turned designs, elaborately embossed and extremely reminiscent of the work done in the late nineteenth century. Made with either an adjustable woven mesh strap, a soldered chain or a finger ring attachment, these vanity cases were manufactured by the Watrous Silver Company.

Finger ring vanity case made with engine-turned designs and an oval enameled medallion picturing a man and a woman dancing, marked R & G Co. Belais 14K white gold front.

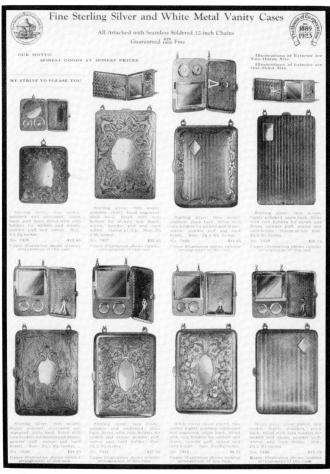

Engraved and embossed vanity cases popular in 1923.

Two vanity cases with attached finger rings, engine-turned designs, enamel and hand-painted decorations. The case on the left is marked R & G Co.; the case on the right is marked F M Co. (Finberg Manufacturing Company, Attleboro, Massachusetts).

Sterling silver vanity cases offered for sale in 1923 from The Ft. Dearborn Watch and Clock Company.

Left—Oval-shaped enameled vanity case with hand-painted flowers, marked Elgin American. Right—Cloisonné enameled vanity case fitted with powder and rouge wells, marked Evans Tap Sift, Pat. 1928.

Goldtone and black enamel vanity case fitted with powder and rouge compartments, marked "le Début Richard Hudnut."

Vanity cases were commonly engraved, embossed, engine-turned, hammered, hand painted or studded with gemstones. Enameling was extremely tasteful and different types of enameling were utilized on sterling silver as well as other metals. Cloisonné and champlevé techniques were two of the most popular types used.

Similar to jewelry and other fashionable accessories, vanity cases were available in all materials and price ranges appealing to the society belle as well as to the working girl. The society belle on both sides of the Atlantic often had her vanity cases commissioned by fine jewelers to be made of gold or platinum and mounted with precious stones. This elite type of evening vanity case was often referred to as a *minaudi*ère. Usually taking the form of an oblong, oval or square-shaped receptacle, the *minaudi*ère was hand carried or suspended by a short chain or silk cord. This elite vanity style was made popular by Van Cleef & Arpels. Many other fine jewelers including, Cartier, Bulgari, Tiffany, Lacloche Frères, Marzo, Chaumet, and Alexandre Marchak, among a few of the most prominent, manufactured these cases as well.

Genuine hand-painted cloisonné enameled compact with swivel-style handle in original velvet lined presentation box.

Fine octagonal-shaped cloisonné enameled double vanity case with movable handle made by the Finberg Manufacturing Company, marked F M Co.

Pink enameled compact with inside sifter for loose powder. *Her Own Place*.

Inside view of chrome and enamel double vanity case made by Volupté.

Chromium-plated vanity case with enamel medallion further enriched with hand-painted flower basket and engine-turned designs, marked O.F.B.Co.

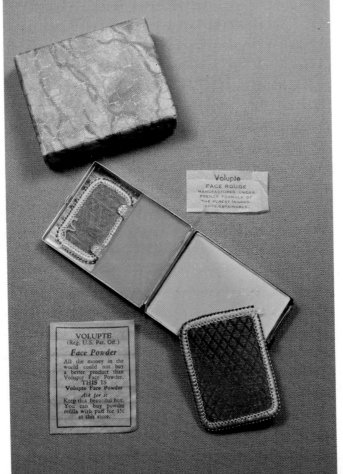

Unusual lighter-shaped perfume atomizer made of chromium plate, black enamel and accented with marcasite-set flower basket, marked Evans ATARMIST.

Minaudière made of gilded sterling in ornate openwork design accented with genuine rubies and sapphires, marked Roma, Sterling. *Her Own Place*.

Inside view of gilded sterling minaudière showing compartments for powder, rouge, lipstick and large mirror.

Exquisite vanity case set with rubies and diamonds made by Tiffany & Company, *Harper's Bazaar*, August, 1936.

TIFFANY & CO.

JEWELERS SILVERSMITHS STATIONERS

FIFTH AVENUE & 37TH STREET, NEW YORK

GOLD BRACELET $225, DIAMOND WRIST WATCH $190, GOLD, TOPAZ AND DIAMOND RING $50, DIAMOND AND SAPPHIRE BAND RING $180, GOLD AND DIAMOND CLIPS $1600 THE PAIR, GOLD CLIP $50, PENNANT SHAPED PLATINUM AND DIAMOND CLIP $190, GOLD AND DIAMOND BRACELET $960, GOLD BRACELET WITH TWO REMOVABLE CABOCHON EMERALD AND DIAMOND CLIPS $550; GOLD AND SILVER VANITY-CASE SET WITH RUBIES AND DIAMONDS $370, SILK BAG WITH SILVER GILT FRAME $39

GOLD JEWELRY, EARRINGS $33 THE PAIR, LINK BRACELET $75, BRACELET SET WITH CARNELIANS $82, BROOCH $19, WRIST WATCH $70; GOLD, PLATINUM AND DIAMOND RING $340; BROCADE PURSE $6.50; VANITY CASE OF STERLING SILVER WITH GOLD AND LACQUER $50, LIPSTICK $27, CIGARETTE CASE TO MATCH, NOT ILLUSTRATED, $72

Jewelry and fashion accessories by Tiffany & Company advertised in *Vogue*, March 1, 1936.

At a recent auction, a gold and enamel vanity case, made by Van Cleef & Arpels in 1925, sold for over $7000. A similar case, designed by Cartier in 1925, sold for $5500. Both cases were decorated with *chinoiserie* enamel designs and suspended by baton link chains with finger ring attachments.

During the Art Deco period, the high class vanity case was also known as a *necessaire* and the fine jewelers were able to capture and interpret the essence of this period with wonderful examples made of gold, platinum, diamonds, rubies, emeralds, sapphires, mother of pearl, onyx, jade, nephrite, cinnabar and lapis lazuli. Oriental motifs were extremely fashionable at that time, displaying eastern techniques such as enamel and lacquer.

Necessaire made of sterling silver which has been engraved with engine-turned designs. The top is decorated with delicate enamel work and attached to a black cord and lipstick tube. The inside is fitted with compartments for powder, rouge and a cylindrical receptacle for holding cigarettes which is concealed beneath long black and white silk fringes. This elegant necessaire was made by Foster & Bailey and marked F & B.

Goldtone compact with paisley ornamentation designed for holding loose face powder by Revlon. The case was designed by Van Cleef & Arpels.

Four Art Deco vanities fashioned in chrome and enamel.

Under the constant influence of fine designers and jewelry houses, many factories and smaller companies copied and adapted to these styles. Less expensive materials were used so that the working girl could obtain similar versions of a glamourous accessory at affordable prices. As demand grew, certain companies specifically involved in manufacturing watch cases broadened their horizons and began manufacturing vanity cases and compacts. These popular accessories now became a major part of the fashion scene. The Elgin American Manufacturing Company, located in Elgin, Illinois and The Wadsworth Company, located in Dayton, Kentucky were two of the most well known.

Square compact made by The Wadsworth Watch Case Company, Dayton, Kentucky, circa 1947.

Elgin American brushed goldtone compact decorated with modernistic ornament consisting of rhinestones and molded imitation sapphires, emeralds and rubies.

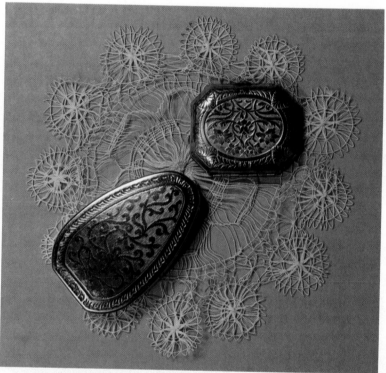

Egg-shaped double vanity case made of chromium plate with added enamel ornamentation, marked "Fianceé, Woodworth, Pat. April 24-Aug 14, 1917." Ornate octagonal double vanity marked "Karess, Woodworth, NY—Paris, Pat. #1570382."

22¢

Metal Vanity Case with Compact Powder

36 T 780—Attractive in appearance and of convenient size to carry in purse or hand bag. Gold Color Metal Vanity Case with compact powder and powder puff for only 22¢. Mirror inside cover. White, flesh or brunette powder. State color . . . . . . **22¢**
Postage 1¢ extra.

Metal vanity case advertised in The National Cloak and Suit Company catalogue, circa 1925.

In 1925, vanity cases of black, jade, red, powder blue and amber-colored celluloid were suspended from short ribbons and worn from the wrist. Long *sautoir* ribbons were also attached to small round vanity cases which resembled watches. This type was conveniently worn around the neck.

In the 1928/1929 National Bellas Hess catalogue, a vanity case made of heavy celluloid with a "Lucky Elephant" painted in a raised design on the front was offered for ninety-eight cents. This particular novelty appealed to women because it was designed to open from both sides. One side held compartments for rouge and face powder while the opposite side revealed a compartment for small change or maybe a handkerchief. It had a silk handle and a long tassel which concealed a lipstick tube. This delightful vanity case was available in red, black or jade-colored celluloid.

Novelty celluloid purse mirrors were extremely popular in the early Twentieth Century. This trio displays actual tinted photographs of three sisters dressed in their finest and proud as peacocks!

38568U

Compact Vanity Case in an antique Green Gold finish, studded with colored stones set in rich ornamentations. Contains Powder Compact, Powder Puff, Rouge Compact, Rouge Puff, Lipstick in holder, and Mirror. Size 2⅝ x 2¼ inches. Has chain handle..... **$3.00**

Jeweled vanity case, circa 1927.

Top—Chrome compact with pie-shaped wedges revealing Paris scenes and people, marked Evening in Paris, Bourjois, Paris—N Y. Center Left—Octagonal-shaped double vanity made of nickel plate over brass with engraved ornamentation, marked Houbigant. Center Right—Double vanity case made of chrome and enamel with Wedgewood-style medallion, marked Dorothy Gray, Fifth Avenue. Bottom—Large flapjack compact with engine-turned designs enriched with navy blue enamel, marked Rex Fifth Avenue.

Brass compact with embossed floral borders enriched with enamel and center celluloid medallion with figural transfer, marked Made in USA, circa 1935. Small celluloid compact with figural transfer on lid, Made in France.

Three brass compacts decorated with
scenic transfers on celluloid lids. The
large compact was patented in 1935;
the small compact is marked Yardley,
London.

Vanity cases and compacts featured in
the Jason Weiler and Sons catalogue,
circa 1927.

Top Left—Gold-plated Twin Compact,
marked "Gardenia, Richard Hudnut,
Pat. Apr 4-22, Jan 2-23 Pats. Pend."
Top Right—Small rouge compact,
marked "Marvelous, Richard Hudnut."
Bottom Left—Double vanity, marked
"Three Flowers, Richard Hudnut."
Bottom Right—Gold-plated DuBarry
compact by Richard Hudnut.

La Mode
FALL COMPACTS

These very interesting and intriguing new
shapes are meeting with signal success,
everywhere. As predicted, this will be a
great season for compacts—the early
trade more than proves this forecast.

The R. & G. lines for Fall are replete with
a whole host of novel, clever patterns and
shapes. Nowhere else will you see such
decidedly different and appealing
patterns. The entire series, including
the "Annette," the "Clarice" and the
"Camille," are equipped with spring catch
which releases at slight pressure of finger.
They all retail at a moderate price.

The "Camille"—Patent Pending

The "Camille" compact by R & G
advertised in The Keystone,
September, 1929.

Vanity case, lipstick and cigarette case by Elgin American advertised in 1929.

Two enameled compacts made of sterling silver decorated with openwork flower baskets, also hand engraved, marked Made In Austria.

Sterling silver double vanity with finger ring attachment by F & B advertised in *The Keystone*, September, 1929.

Compacts

In 1908, Sears, Roebuck & Co. offered a small silver-plated pocketbook toilet case with a hinged cover and an inside mirror. It was fitted with a small swans down puff with a celluloid ring handle. Described as "being small enough to carry in the pocketbook" and "just the article for parties, traveling, etc...", this toilet case sold for nineteen cents. By the next decade, this small and round case, which housed loose face powder, puff and mirror became known as a compact. Again, fine jewelers made these decorative little jewels in precious materials when commissioned by wealthy aristocrats while modestly priced examples were available in less expensive materials and sold in department stores, drug stores and through mail-order catalogues.

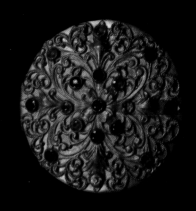

Brass compact with ornate openwork pattern further accented with bezel-set imitation stones.

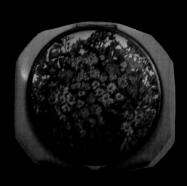

Two elegant compacts completely encrusted with tiny seed beads on both sides and further embellished with an exquisite enameled portrait medallion positioned in the center surrounded by seed pearls, European.

Vanity cases made of sterling silver offered for sale in 1920 from the John V. Farwell Company.

Pink plastic compact with flower basket design on foil-type paper sold by John Wanamaker in the 1930s.

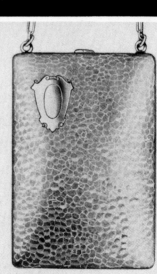

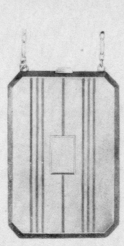

J33698—Vanity Case: extra heavy sterling silver; hammered; sterling silver fittings throughout as in illustration J33666 (except has no pencil); mirror with memo. tablet on back, and place for powder, 2 coin holders and card compartment; size 3½x2½ inches.
....Each 32.50

J33699—Vanity Case: heavy sterling silver; polished and engraved; sterling silver fittings throughout as in illustration J33696; (except has no pencil); mirror with memo. tablet on back; 2 coin holders and card compartment; size 3½x2½ inches; this vanity is same size as J33695; although cut is smaller. Each 30.00

J33700—Vanity Case: heavy sterling silver; hammered front; French gray finish; burnished back; inside same as illustration J33696; (except has no pencil); size 3½x2½ inches ....Each 26.50

Hand engraved compact, marked 800 Silver, Italy. *John Morse Jr..*

As popularity for this little accessory escalated, many new materials were put to use. Sterling silver was used in abundance in addition to brass, aluminum, gunmetal, nickel, gilt, crystal and plastics. Compacts were plated, painted, polished, beaded, brushed, chased, enameled, engraved, fluted or garnished with gemstones. Leather, such as pig skin, ostrich, alligator, snakeskin and calfskin appeared, and on rare occasions, fur covered compacts were produced. Novelties included compacts in the shape of praying hands, guitars, pianos, books, fans, suitcases, hats, hearts, hand mirrors, cameras, horseshoes, crowns and animals. Working watches were set right into the tops of square compacts while round compacts were made to resemble pocket watches. Compacts were designed to light up or play music when opened. Photographs of famous and even not-so-famous people were mounted on compacts while other examples displayed pictures or paintings of scenic places and reproductions of classical art. Petit-point compacts were highly fashionable and imported from Austria and Germany. Tiny compacts were tucked neatly into the tops of large hatpins and these "vanity hatpins" were popular from the Gay Nineties' until the first world war. Compacts were placed in bracelets, lockets and rings and were concealed in purse frames and walking canes. So necessary had they become that women were considered not completely dressed without them!

Novelty compacts, including the tango-chain varieties, offered for sale in 1935.

Round compact cases with enamel ornamentation, circa 1935.

Compact made of sterling silver, all hand engraved with bird designs and monogram shield. *Her Own Place*.

Watchcase enameled double vanity, marked Timepact, Made in USA, circa 1930s.

"Jingle Bells" double vanity, book-shaped compact case and Persian style compact made by Coty.

Celluloid compact with Petit Point under a clear plastic sheet bordered in brass with engraved designs.

Compact decorated with "Genuine Hand Made Petitpoint" by Schildkraut, 1650 stitches per square inch.

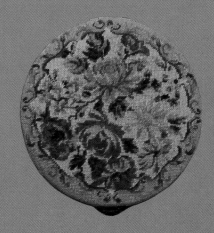

Silver-plated compact with floral transfer made by Elgin American.

Two goldtone watchcase compacts made by Evans Case Company, circa 1940s.

Square scenic compact, marked Gwenda, Made in England; Rectangular compact, enameled blue, resembling a postcard, Pat. #1883793, Made in USA, circa 1932-33; Enameled compact with classical scene, marked Shields.

Brass compact with celluloid medallion, alligator design and rhinestone enrichment.

Square black enameled compact with hand painted floral designs, marked Volupté.

Large compact made of gold overlay with etched designs and plastic warrior head in high relief accompanied by original pouch, marked Maravilla.

Sterling silver compact enameled yellow and blue enameled compact both marked F M Co. (Finberg Manufacturing Company); Small locket-style enameled compact made of sterling silver is unmarked. *Her Own Place*.

Oblong, square, oval and octagonal-shaped compacts were also extremely common in the 1920s. Tinsel metallic brocade covered large flap-jack compacts. Florentine leather with 22K gold embossing covered square and rectangular compacts. Beads and pearls were embroidered on gold lamé compacts. Lusterful enamel with oriental damascene was quite stylish in the thirties and the forties along with compacts enriched with silver fleck enamel. Speckled Lucite compacts and matching purse accessories became the rage in the 1950s. Manufacturers produced complete fashion accessory sets in Lucite including carryalls, compacts, purse combs, perfume bottles, cigarette cases, lighters, lipstick tubes, lipvues, pillboxes, picture frames and credit card cases in a large array of pastel shades and made in many different shapes and sizes. Curry Arts of Scranton, Pennsylvania and Zell Fifth Avenue of New York City were two prime manufacturers of this particular type of compact.

Octagonal-shaped compact with hand engraved top depicting bamboo and leaf designs, marked 950 Silver.

Square chromium-plated compact with scenic "Rio" fashioned from a butterfly wing, made by Coty.

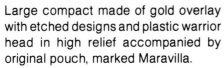

Large flapjack compact designed to hold loose powder made of celluloid with an engraved silver-plated top in original pouch, marked Rex Fifth Avenue.

Gilded brass compact with figural transfer and hand painting on clear plastic lid.

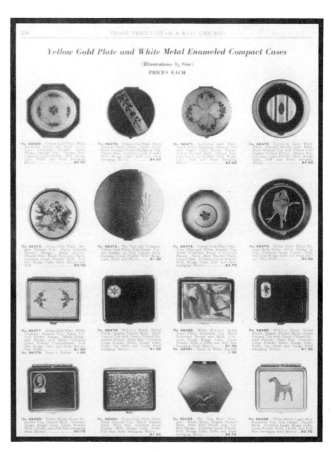

A variety of compacts popular in 1935.

Two oval compacts studded with tiny rhinestones by K & K; two goldtone compacts studded with multi-colored stones by Lin-Bren.

Variety of Lucite fashion accessories to include lipvue, comb, perfume vials, compact and billfold.

Four pieces of yellow speckled Lucite consisting of oval compact, flashlight, mini-carryall and purse comb by Curry Arts.

Octagonal-shaped double vanity case with green celluloid top decorated with an Eastern Star pattern enriched with rhinestones, marked Gamsborough.

Black speckled Lucite compact, billfold and lipvue.

A variety of compacts topped with speckled Lucite by Curry Arts, Scranton, Pa. (This type of Lucite is also referred to as confetti Lucite.)

Speckled Lucite fashion accessories by Curry Arts.

Compacts and lipvues made of speckled Lucite by Curry Arts.

Pink speckled Lucite fashion accessories by Curry Arts.

Five pieces of yellow speckled Lucite by Curry Arts.

Fashion accessories made of speckled Lucite by Curry Arts.

Six piece matched set of gray confetti Lucite by Curry Arts.

Ten pieces of speckled or confetti Lucite made by Curry Arts, Scranton, Pa.

Flowers embedded in clear Lucite decorate this compact and pillbox.

Six piece set consisting of three compacts, lipstick tube, perfume vial and folding comb made of a clear Lucite placed over a leopard-type cloth, unmarked.

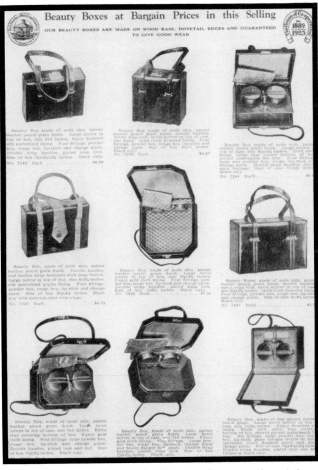

Mole skin Beauty Boxes offered for sale in 1923.

Blue and black Bakelite manicure set accented with rhinestones and silk tassel fitted with four tiny manicure tools, marked Germany. The outside of the case reads: "Souvenir of Canada."

Materials and designs

Leather was a favorite material employed when manufacturing vanity or beauty boxes which fitted a large beveled mirror, coin purse and three or more metal cases designed to hold powder, rouge and lipstick. In 1923, a triplicate mirror beauty box was featured in a mail-order catalogue. Made of genuine cobra grain leather, it contained three beveled mirrors, two shirred pockets and five additional fittings: powder box, rouge box, pin box, lipstick and change purse. It retailed for $18.00. For half the price, a mole skin beauty box, fitted with large mirror, powder box, rouge box, lipstick, change purse and electric light attachment was available. Most beauty boxes were equipped with a lock and key being very practical when traveling.

Mother-of-pearl was abundant in the manufacture of traditional round and square compacts as well as other fashion accessories including purse mirrors, carryalls, cigarette cases, lighters and much more. Pierced work, checkerboard patterns and inlaid designs were quite common. Mother-of-pearl compacts were also studded with rhinestones, enriched with pearls or hand painted. Mother-of-pearl compacts and accessories became so popular that imitations began to flood the market. In the 1930s, referred to as "pearl effect", imitation mother of pearl was made of plastic.

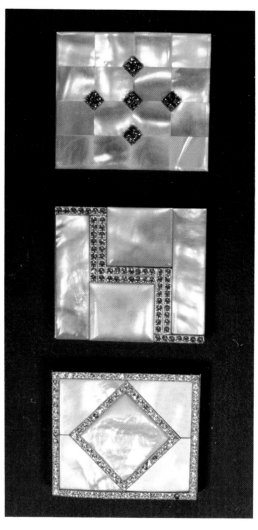

Three mother-of-pearl compacts enriched with rhinestones made by Ansico.

Genuine mother-of-pearl accessories by Wiesner of Miami, the Shell Compact Company and Ansico.

Matched set consisting of triple vanity, powder compact and small portable ashtray made of decorated mother-of-pearl.

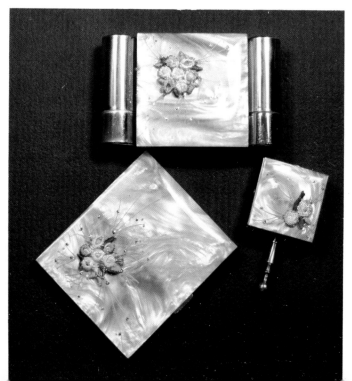

Three goldtone compacts enriched with square tiles of genuine mother-of-pearl.

A variety of 1950s fashion accessories made of real and imitation mother-of-pearl (genuine mother-of-pearl is colder to the touch and displays traces of color).

Book-shaped compact made of inlaid mother-of-pearl by Ansico circa 1950s; Lighter-shaped compact made of inlaid mother-of-pearl with goldtone opening mechanism on top, Pat'd. 1932.

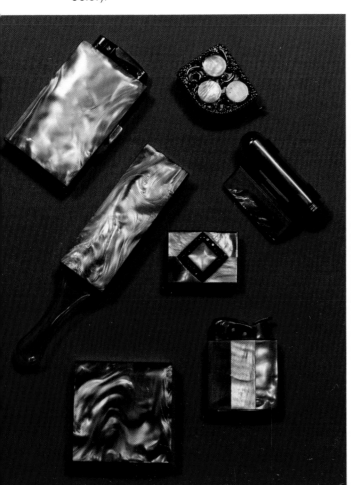

Matched set consisting of compact, charge plate holder and perfume vial made of inlaid mother-of-pearl.

A pierced design decorates this mother-of-pearl compact; small compact made of mother-of-pearl with carved rose rendered in high relief by Ansico.

Imitation mother-of-pearl fashion accessories to include lipvue, compact and cigarette lighter by Marhill.

Matched set consisting of compact and rectangular cigarette case made of imitation mother-of-pearl further embellished with glitter and hand painting.

Imitation mother-of-pearl costume accessories to include folding purse comb, mirror and contact lens case, marked Marhill, circa 1960s.

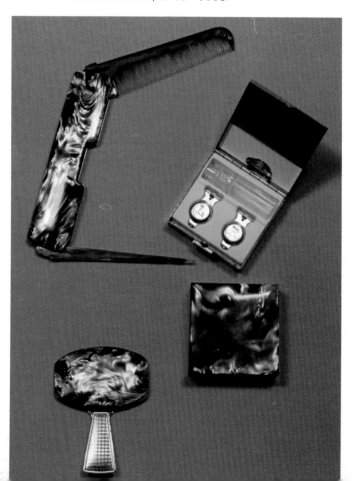

In 1929, a wonderful and extremely colorful display of compacts were manufactured by the J.M. Fisher Company of Attleboro, Massachusetts. This particular line was designed to commemorate fifty years of business for the company. The compacts varied in shape as well as size. Romantic and classical themes were rendered in enamel as well as those depicting the very modernistic tone of the Art Deco period.

In the same year, The Evans Case Company from North Attleboro, Massachusetts created their new line of compacts primarily designed in the Art Deco style with bold colors and geometric patterns rendered in enamel. This very popular company also manufactured cigarette cases, lighters, mesh vanity bags and costume jewelry.

Following page:
Enameled vanity cases with chair handles and finger ring attachments made by the JM Fisher Company advertised in *The Keystone*, September, 1929.

Beautiful enameled vanity cases with finger ring attachments made by the JM Fisher Company, advertised in *The Keystone*, September, 1929.

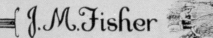
ILLUSTRATIONS FULL SIZE
ALL CASES WHITE FINISH AND FRONTS ENAMEL PAINTED

F109 $4.50 ea.
The Bather. Fitted with mirror, rouge
and loose powder sifter.

F110 $4.50 ea.
Old Fashioned Girl. Enameled both
sides and has invisible joint. Fitted
with mirror, rouge and loose powder
sifter.

F111 $4.50 ea.
Red Boat. Fitted with mirror, rouge
and loose powder sifter.

F112 $4.88 ea.
Apple Blossoms. Fitted with mirror,
loose powder sifter, rouge and lipstick.

F113 $5.25 ea.
The Ivy Vine Girls. Fitted with mirror,
loose powder sifter, rouge, lipstick and
perfume stick.

F114 $4.88 ea.
Fairy Pond Lilies. Fitted with mirror,
loose powder sifter, rouge and lipstick.

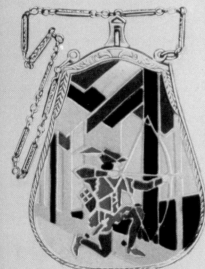  

F115 $5.25 ea.
Robinhood. Fitted with mirror, loose
powder sifter, rouge, lipstick and perfume stick.

F116 $4.88 ea.
Japanese Scene. Fitted with mirror,
loose powder sifter, rouge and lipstick.

F117 $5.25 ea.
Parrot. Fitted with mirror, loose pow-
der sifter, rouge, lipstick and perfume
stick.

THE MOST FOR THE MONEY   FOR OVER FIFTY YEARS

REG. U.S. PAT. OFF.   AND CANADA

Exquisite enameled vanity cases made by Evans advertised in *The Keystone*, September, 1929.

EVANS

E1550—White finish, engine turned design with French enamel decoration, fitted with mirror, loose powder container and rouge, French enamel lipstick handle. $3.00 ea.

E1552—White finish, thin model, engine turned brocade design in modernistic pattern, with hand painted French enamel decoration, flexible handle, fitted with mirror, loose powder container and rouge. $3.75 ea.

E1551—White finish, thin watch case model, engine turned design with French enamel decoration and contrasting border, fitted with mirror, loose powder container. $1.50 ea.

E1553—White finish, thin model, French enamel front, contrasting colors, flexible handle, fitted with large mirror, loose powder container and rouge. $5.52 ea.

E1554—White finish, thin knife edge watch case model. French enamel cover with genuine Marcasite set decoration fitted with mirror, loose powder container and rouge. $6.40 ea.

E1555—White finish, thin model, French enamel front with decorative placque, fitted with large mirror, loose powder container and rouge, French enamel lipstick handle. $5.25 ea.

E1556—White finish, thin model, French enamel front, contrasting colors, fitted with mirror, loose powder container and rouge, finger ring and chain. $4.50 ea.

E1557—White finish, thin knife edge model, French enamel cover, with decorative placque, fitted with mirror, loose powder container and rouge, French enamel lipstick handle. $6.75 ea.

E1558—White finish, thin model French enamel front in modernistic design, fitted with mirror, loose powder container and rouge, flexible handle. $5.25 ea.

E1559—Green gold finish, thin model genuine Viennese enamel front and back, with genuine hand engraved Viennese enamel cover, fitted with mirror, loose powder container and rouge. $12.75 ea.

E1560—White finish, thin knife edge model, French enamel front and back with French enamel cover in contrasting colors, finger ring and chain. $9.00 ea.

E1561—Green gold finish, thin knife edge model, genuine Viennese enamel front and back with genuine hand engraved Viennese enamel cover, fitted with mirror, loose powder container and rouge. $15.00 ea.

Illustrations four-fifth size.

The LINE with the STERLING TOUCH

Prices are retail—Order now thru your jobber—Subject to Keystone Discount

EVANS CASE CO., North Attleboro, Mass.

Modernistic Art Deco motifs are clearly displayed on these colorful vanity cases made by Evans, *The Keystone*, September, 1929.

Round compact with tri-colored basket weave pattern, marked Evans, Sterling; Goldtone compact with alternating segments of black enamel, marked Majestic.

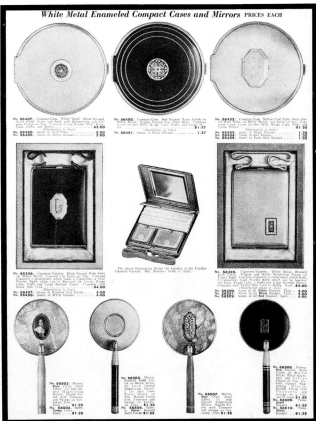

Compacts, mirrors and Cigarette-Vanettes offered for sale in 1935.

Genuine hand painted cloisonné embellishes this compact made by Evans.

In 1932, Elizabeth Arden created a new line of compact-lipstick ensembles which were made to "enhance summertime frocks." Colors like jade, chariot red, maroon red, new blue, silver, black and white were available to choose from. Besides the actual cosmetics that were color harmonized, the containers which held cosmetics were also being made to coordinate with specific outfits.

In the summer of 1936, the Volupté Company of Fifth Avenue in New York City created a new line of compacts and cigarette cases designed with colorful, embossed vegetables on white enameled cases. Turnips, beets, carrots and corn created unusual themes and novel fashion accessories. They were sold in fine department stores for $5.00 each. Fruit and vegetable themes were also quite common in jewelry design during this decade.

Fob compacts by Evans, *Harper's Bazaar*, June, 1936.

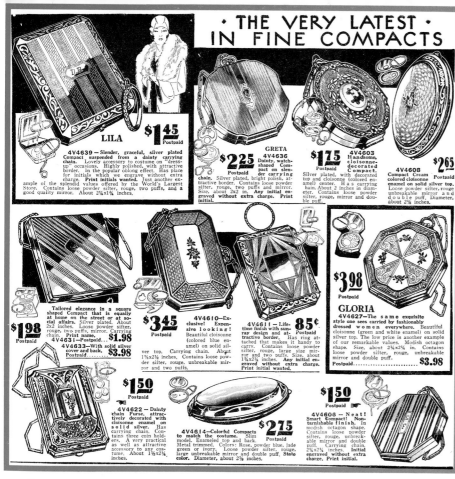
Compacts and vanity cases offered for sale in the 1930 Sears catalogue.

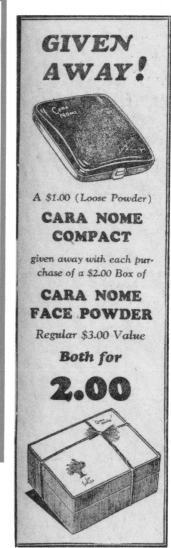
"Cara Nome" compact featured as a Drug Store Give-a-way in June, 1930.

Two sterling silver hand engraved compacts, marked Wadsworth.

Black and silver enameled compacts by Elizabeth Arden, "Ardenette", circa 1930.

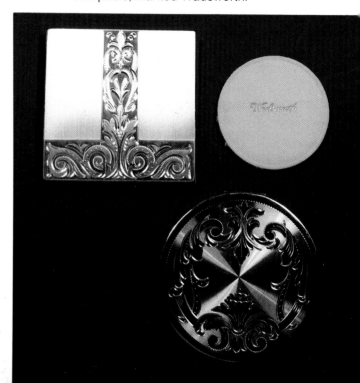

Flower basket compact by Houbigant sold in John Wanamaker's Department Store in Philadelphia, June 10, 1930.

Majestic silver-plated basket weave compact; sterling silver compact, hand engraved in sun ray pattern marked, Elizabeth Arden; Round silver-plated compact with "Cracker Barrel" scene rendered in high relief, marked S & F; round silver-plated compact with engraved designs, marked Made in Switzerland.

Volupté vanities and cigarette cases, *Harper's Bazaar*, April, 1936.

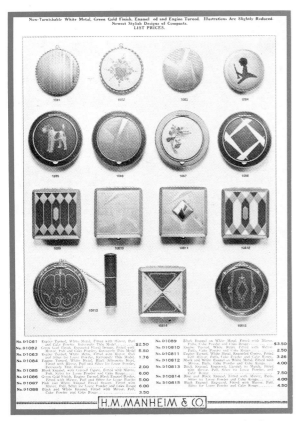

Lovely assortment of enameled compacts and vanity cases popular in 1933.

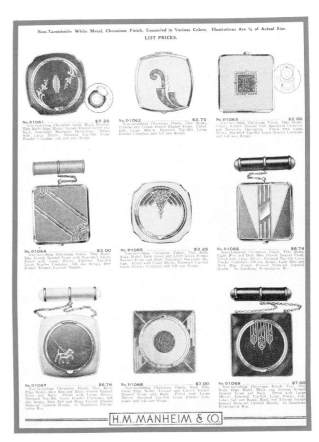

Enameled compacts sold in 1933, H.M. Manheim Company.

Yellow gold plate and white metal enameled compacts, circa 1935.

Square black enameled compact enriched with a cluster of multi-colored stones, marked Volupté.

In the same year, Yardley introduced its new *Mirror-Pact* compact. This particular novelty, which opened like a slide rule, resembled a miniature vanity table. This was also the year that the first raffia compact was designed for summer wear. Imported from Paris by Bonwit Teller, it was made slightly larger but half as thick as a pack of cigarettes. It contained a well for loose powder and a swans down puff. This compact retailed for $7.50.

Round compact cases, sometimes called loose powder pouches, were similar in appearance to the earlier Tam O' Shanter coin purses. They were usually two inches in diameter with exquisite, enameled tops and the bottoms were made of leather or metal mesh. Evans was responsible for manufacturing a tremendous amount of loose powder pouches in the 1930s.

Yardley's "Mirror-Pact" compact featured in *Harper's Bazaar* in 1936.

Yardley vanity set featured in *Vogue*, February 15, 1938.

Three loose powder pouches with goldtone mesh bottoms made by Evans.

Assortment of compacts featured in the Sears catalogue in 1937.

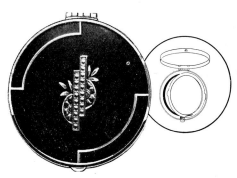

COMPACT

No. D13312 .... **$1.00**
Non-Tarnishing, Chromium Finish, Thin Model, Black French Enamel Front with Simulated Marcasite Decoration. Fitted with Large Mirror and Loose Powder Container. Illustration 2/3 Size.

No. D13313 COMPACT **$1.13**
Loose Powder Pouch, Non-Tarnishing, Chromium Finish with Black French Enamel Top, Soft Genuine Blue Leather Pouch. Fitted with Large Mirror, Large Velour Puff and Sifter. Illustration Actual Size.

No. D13314 COMPACT **$2.00**
Non-Tarnishing, Chromium Finish, Thin Watch Case Model, Black French Enamel Front with Simulated Marcasite Decoration. Fitted with Large Mirror, Loose Powder Container and Rouge. French Enamel Lipstick Handle. Illustration ¾ Size.

Loose powder pouches and tango chain compacts featured in the H.M. Manheim catalogue in 1933.

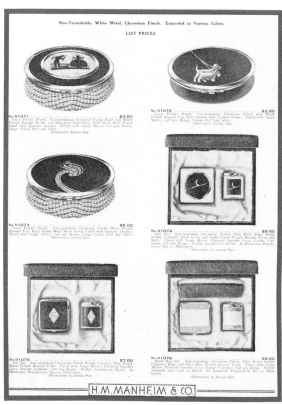

Loose powder pouches and compact sets offered for sale in 1933.

Gold-, silver- and nickel-plated rosary compact cases.

208—Small Rosary Carrying Case and s; gold filled case and beads; diameter se ⅞ inch....................Each 7.50
209—As above; sterling silver case and s ....Each 8.50

J31210—Rosary Carrying Case; nickel silver; French gray finish; velvet pocket for rosary inside; size 3x2¼ inches....Each 4.00

J31211—Rosary Carrying Case and Beads; nickel silver; polished; silk lined; one pocket for rosary and one for coins; 2⅜x2¼ inches; complete with rosary; amethyst beads......
....Each 9.00
J31212—As above; case only; sterling silver; will hold medium size rosary.Each 13.50

Rosary carrying cases offered for sale by the John V. Farwell Company in 1920.

Three loose powder pouches with silvertone mesh bottoms and enameled tops made by Evans.

In 1937, a very elegant line of compacts and cigarette cases were manufactured by Volupté depicting motifs inspired by "Imperial Russia" and the wonderful enamel work of Fabergé. The compacts illustrated hand work techniques which were rendered in "brushed platinum and gold finishes." As with other Volupté compacts, they were sold in fine department stores everywhere.

"Imperial Russia" collection by Volupté featured in *Harper's Bazaar*, October, 1937.

VOLUPTÉ

Presents **MASSIVE DESIGNS** *in*
Compacts and Cigarette Cases

In the same year, another New York City company known as Henriette, manufactured compacts and cigarette cases made of gold or platinum-finished metal designed in exquisite cutwork patterns. These designs were specifically created for evening wear. Two years later, Henriette offered black and gold enameled compacts and matching cigarette cases "topped with a glittering jewel-studded nosegay to compliment the season's elegance."

Deeply cut, hand-engine turning, a note strongly sponsored by the famous French jewelers, gives this compact and cigarette case ensemble its new look of importance. Volupté presents a series of these massive, modern designs in gold or silver finish to complement the dramatic richness of Winter costumes. In outstanding stores.

VOLUPTÉ INC., 347 FIFTH AVENUE, NEW YORK

Compact and cigarette case by Volupté, *Harper's Bazaar*, November, 1936.

● **Cutwork Cigarette Case,** satin-finish metal plated in gold or platinum. Engagingly permits a lady to see at a glance how many cigarettes she has.

● **Cutwork Powder Case,** to match the cigarette case above. Here the cutwork pattern is handsomely silhouetted against black velvet.

Lovely ensemble consisting of cigarette case and matching compact by Henriette, *Harper's Bazaar*, November, 1937.

BLACK BEAUTIES *by* Henriette

AT CHRISTMAS COUNTERS OF BETTER STORES

Sleek tributes to your unerring taste, and her sophisticated charm. Gold-and-black enamelled compact and matching cigarette case, topped with a glittering, jewel-studded nosegay to complement the season's elegance. She'll carry them proudly to tea, to cocktails, to dinner.

HENRIETTE, INC., 385 FIFTH AVENUE, N. Y. • 35 EAST WACKER DRIVE, CHICAGO

"Black Beauties" by Henriette, *Harper's Bazaar*, December, 1939.

der Cases as
Costume Accessories

● For British tweeds. An entirely new finish. "Dover Mist," finely grained in misty combinations like the new tweeds. Plain enamel bands. Black with white, green with London tan, blue with white. Jack-in-the-Box case.

Jack-in-the-Box, newest of Henriette's ideas, will be hailed by women who like "plenty of powder" yet a light, thin case. Like all Henriette's things, it is exquisitely executed — white leather Jack-in-the-Box sides, a luxurious swan's-down puff, and a variety of smart cases designed to accent fall fashions.

This is perhaps Henriette's most important contribution to the whole question of powder cases for smart women. There are colors and styles for every costume. You'll be able to select one for every bag you have.

Jack-in-the-Box cases, from $3.00, as well as many other attractive models, are featured at leading department stores. Henriette, Inc., 385 Fifth Ave., New York.

by Henriette

● For the first dark fall dress. Gleaming satin-finished metal in smart fluted design. Jack-in-the-Box case. Very distinguished with jewelled clip.

Fashion accessories by Henriette, *Harper's Bazaar*, October, 1937.

Oval triple vanity case, nickel-plated over brass, marked Fitch.

Inside view of Fitch triple vanity case.

Double compacts and vanities, which sometimes opened from both sides, were used to hold powder and puff on one side and rouge and puff on the other. Triple vanities contained powder, rouge and lipstick. Edouardo of New York City advertised their line of triple and quadruple vanities in 1929 as the Edouardo "Threesome" which contained face powder, rouge and lip paste; the Edouardo "Foursome" was fitted with powder, rouge, lip paste and imported solid perfume. Another popular triple vanity is the *Trio-ette* by Platé. It is a "powder, rouge and lipstick ensemble" made of "moulded Tenite" fashioned in the shape of a lovely Victorian rose hand mirror. The Trio-ette was in vogue in the 1940s.

Edouardo compacts advertised in 1929.

Edouardo
COMPACTS
Newest Design—Newest Color

Edouardo Compact — black line design on red enamel—in "Threesome" and "Foursome" styles.

Edouardo "Threesome" $2.50

Face Powder: Sun-kissed, Rachel or Flesh
Rouge: Medium or Raspberry
Lippaste: Medium or Raspberry

Edouardo "Foursome" $3.75

(With extra Powder Refill and Puff —$4.00).
Face Powder—Rouge—Lippaste—Imported Solid Perfume (as in Bag-Dabs).
Shades: same as "Threesome"

"Threesome" and "Foursome" Compacts may also be obtained in our regular silver-plated design.

PARFUMS
Edouardo
300 Fourth Ave., New York

Top—Wadsworth triple vanity made of silvertone and goldtone metal and three raised flowers set with rhinestones. Bottom—Double vanity with checkerboard design, marked Renard, NY.

Top—Rectangular-shaped enameled triple vanity case with chrome interior fitted with compartments for powder, rouge and lipstick, marked Bourjois. Bottom—Goldtone and black enamel double vanity, marked "By Vanstyle."

"Trio-ette" by Platé molded plastic triple vanity case made to resemble a hand mirror fitted with powder, rouge and lipstick.

36T783—Double Vanity Case of Gold color metal with engraved top. Two compartments inside; one has large compact of face powder with flat puff. Smaller compact of medium rouge with separate puff inside lid; hinged mirror. White, flesh or brunette powder......... Post. 2¢ extra. 98¢

Double vanity case, circa 1925.

Tango-chain compacts, also called lipstick handle compacts, were stylish throughout the Art Deco period. They were usually designed with a square, round or rectangular compact case suspended by one or two chains which were attached to a matching lipstick tube. Most often, tango-chain compacts were decorated in bright enamel with geometric designs enhanced by stylized motifs or delicately styled with hand painting and cloisonné or champlevé enamel.

Commemorative compacts depicting special events were also popular. The 1933 Century of Progress and the 1939 New York World's Fair were two of the most popular themes for which compact manufacturers based their designs. Another variation of a commemorative compact was the "Scarlet O' Hara" compact designed to commemorate the classic movie *Gone With The Wind*. Popular in 1940, and available in three different styles, these compacts were manufactured by Volupté.

In the early forties, obviously inspired by World War II, military cap compacts were sold through Sears for $1.00 each. These plastic novelty compacts, actually depicting specific branches of the military, corresponded in color and style to either the Army, Navy or the Marines. In 1943, a "Gone to War" compact was also available in sterling silver with a gold-plated Air Corps insignia mounted on the top of the case. It was fitted with a powder sifter, puff and mirror. This example retailed for $13.11. The war created a variety of themes upon which manufacturers based their novelty designs and for a time, these compacts were very stylish.

Tango chain triple vanity case made of chrome and green enamel.

Chrome and black enamel double vanity case, Chicago's "A Century of Progress", circa 1933.

Folding purse comb with "Cracker Barrel" design; Art Nouveau brass hand mirror; Silver-plated hand mirror, souvenir of Jamaica.

Many Splendid Styles to Select From

1187R-135 Striking silver stripe on mother-of-pearl. Handsome bronze-like interior with mirror, puff and space for powder.
Retail $2.25

1188R-205 A distinctive cigarette case to match compact. Same silver stripe and pearl combination. Bronze-like interior. Its compactness makes it ideal for evening wear.
Retail $3.50

1190R-135 Natural gold color leaf design on black enameled background with gold tone trim and interior with puff, mirror and space for powder.
Retail $2.25

1191R-75 Smart compact with natural gold color decoration on either white or black enameled case. Specify color wanted.
Retail $1.2

1192R-245 The rounded streamlined case detailed in pink gold and green gold color on natural bronze tone background. Interior has window lid which covers loose powder compartment.
Retail $3.95

1193R-75 Dainty floral decorations on enameled background of pink, black, white or blue. Specify color wanted. Retail $1.25

1194R-450 Various light reflections on this mother-of-pearl case cause a series of beautiful rainbow color effects. The interior is finished in a gold tone and there is ample space for a generous supply of regular or long cigarettes.
Retail $7.50

1195R-340 Compact matches cigarette case. Lovely castle on lake scene. Gold tone interior has separate covered compartment for loose powder.
Retail $5.50

Compacts and cigarette cases featured in the Carson Pirie Scott & Company Jewelry Yearbook, circa 1942.

Square compact enameled blue decorated with US Army insignia. On the inside of this compact, under the lid, is another compartment which opens to reveal a picture of an army soldier.

Raffia Compact.

Heart-shaped goldtone compact with military insignia, marked Hingeco, Made in USA; Plastic Navy hat compact with insignia, marked Henriette. *Ann Marsh.*

Compacts offered for sale in 1942 including the popular watch vanity by Elgin American.

Merry-go-Round Compact.

"He Loves Me, He Loves Me Not" compact, hand painted with side zippered closure, marked Lady Vanity.

In 1946, the merry-go-round compact was offered through Sears and was advertised as the "gayest compact you've ever owned." The case was a gold-colored metal, decorated around the sides with "prancing ponies", and further enriched with a red, white and blue enameled carousel-like top. It retailed for $1.98.

"The greatest improvement in compacts in years" was nationally advertised in 1947 when the "Venus-Ray" was put on the market. This streamlined metal compact contained a light that lit up when opened. It was also fitted with a lipstick, a powder compartment and a perfume vial. Manufactured by the Spotlite Corporation, it retailed for $6.00.

Large compact, enameled green, with raised goldtone designs accompanied by original pouch, marked Elgin American; Red enamel compact with engraved goldtone floral design, marked Elgin American, circa 1946.

Compacts and cigarette cases, Sears, Roebuck and Company, 1946.

The "Venus-Ray" compact was designed to light when opened. It was popular in 1947.

Sterling silver compact decorated with hand engraved Siamese dancer, in original presentation box, marked Made in Siam, Sterling. The box reads: Ed and Joe's Shops, Registered in Thailand, Thailand (Siam) Import Branch, Bangkok. Thailand.

He gave Her a Volupté compact

... Volupté's charming new watchcase compact, "Gay Garden." Gold and silver color with bright rhinestone flowers. About $10*

VOLUPTÉ

Reflects the prettiest faces

Watchcase compact called "Gay Garden" by Volupté, circa 1953.

In the early fifties, Volupté created many different versions of the watchcase compact and each case was given a specific name. For example, the "Morning Glory" was a round compact that was enameled white with a floral design and rhinestone accents. This model, attached to a black silk cord, retailed for $7.50 in 1953. Another variation was made of goldtone or silvertone metal with an embossed floral design further embellished with rhinestones. This watchcase compact, called the "Gay Garden", retailed for $10.00.

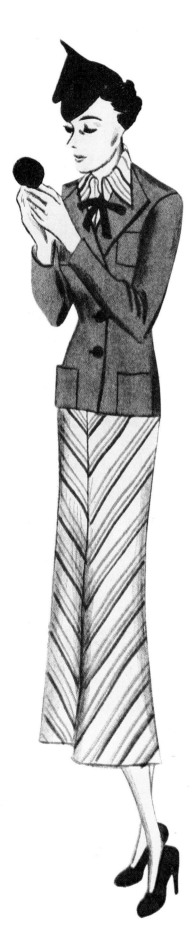

Nickel silver compact with engraved top and floral porcelain medallion, marked Rex Fifth Avenue.

Rectangular compact with celluloid top decorated with figural transfer; Round compact, souvenir of Parliment Square, London, marked Made in Great Britian.

Large celluloid compact with floral transfer on lid, marked Made in USA, Pat. #2163429, circa 1939-40.

Wiesner of Miami also created a line of watchcase compacts in the fifties. They were made of a goldtone metal and decorated with either rhinestones or simulated pearl medallions mounted on the top of the compact. The back of the case had intricate engine-turned designs. A black silk cord was attached to a triangular loop at the opening mechanism. These compacts were fitted with a powder sifter, a puff and mirror. Purple and gold labels, with the words, *Trickettes by Wiesner*, were found on the mirror. This company was also responsible for exquisitely crafting other fashion accessories garnished with hand-set jewels. Complete sets were produced consisting of compacts, lipvues, cigarette cases, lighters, frames, combs, pillboxes and carryalls accompanied by cloth pouches and purple presentation boxes. Trickettes by Wiesner were available in fine department stores and boutiques throughout the United States.

Four goldtone compacts decorated with round medallions of imitation pearls and colored stones, marked "Trickettes" by Wiesner of Miami.

Three watchcase compacts made of a brushed goldtone metal further enriched with rhinestones and imitation pearls and black silk cords, marked "Trickettes" by Wiesner of Miami.

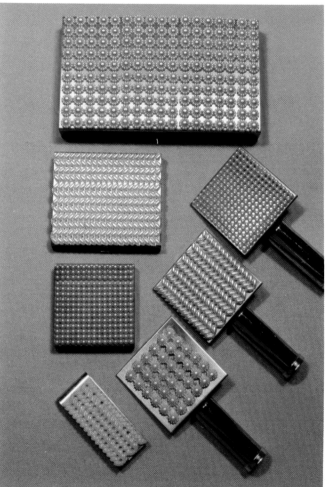

Jeweled fashion accessories made by Wiesner of Miami.

Very elegant fashion accessory set embellished with rhinestones made by Wiesner of Miami.

Imitation pearl topped fashion accessories to include lipvues, carryall and money clip, marked "Trickettes" by Wiesner of Miami.

Elegant five piece jeweled fashion accessory set made of imitation opal and amethyst stones by Wiesner of Miami. The set includes a folding purse comb, two perfume vials, a lipvue and cigarette lighter.

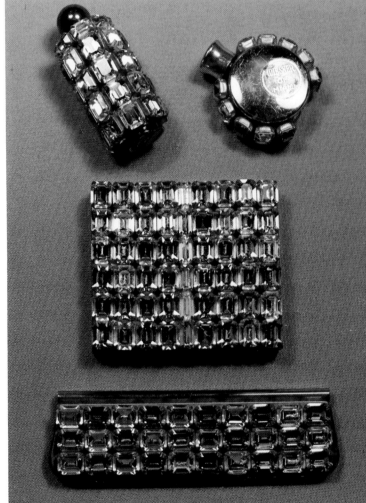

Lovely four piece jeweled fashion accessory set made of clear and light blue rhinestones by Wiesner of Miami. The set includes two perfume vials, compact and folding purse comb.

Black and clear rhinestones embellish this six piece fashion accessory set by Wiesner of Miami.

Aqua-colored rhinestones decorate this five piece fashion accessory set by Wiesner of Miami.

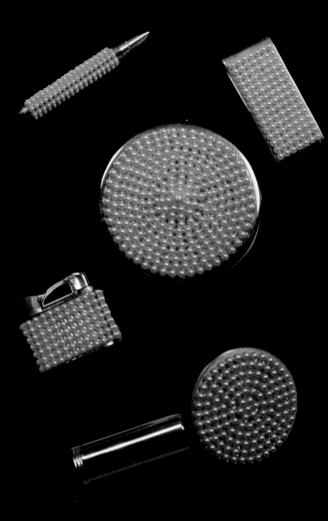

Ensemble of pearl fashion accessories including compact, lipvue, pencil, lighter and money clip by Wiesner of Miami

Two pill boxes and perfume bottle encrusted with imitation pearls and hand set stones by Wiesner of Miami

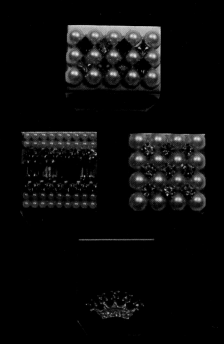

Six jeweled perfume vials, marked
Wiesner of Miami.

Six jeweled lipstick tubes, marked
Wiesner of Miami.

Four jeweled pillboxes decorated with
hand set stones.

Seven pillboxes with hand-set jewels,
unmarked.

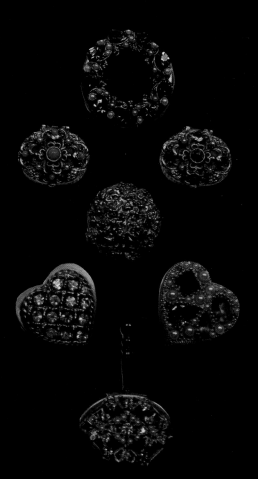

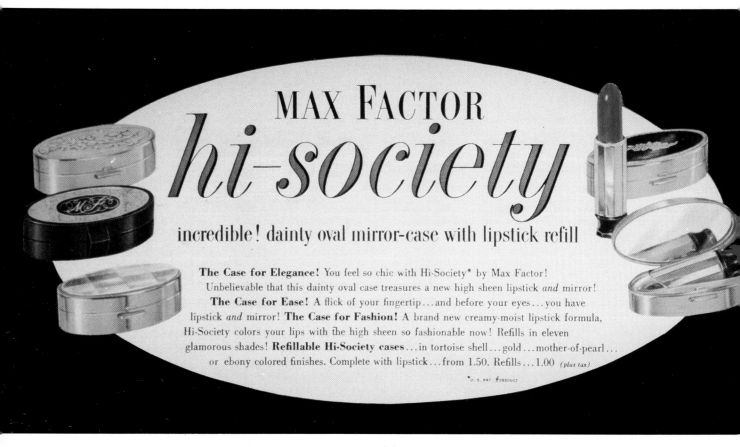

MAX FACTOR
hi-society

incredible! dainty oval mirror-case with lipstick refill

The Case for Elegance! You feel so chic with Hi-Society* by Max Factor! Unbelievable that this dainty oval case treasures a new high sheen lipstick *and* mirror! **The Case for Ease!** A flick of your fingertip...and before your eyes...you have lipstick *and* mirror! **The Case for Fashion!** A brand new creamy-moist lipstick formula, Hi-Society colors your lips with the high sheen so fashionable now! Refills in eleven glamorous shades! **Refillable Hi-Society cases**...in tortoise shell...gold...mother-of-pearl... or ebony colored finishes. Complete with lipstick...from 1.50. Refills...1.00 *(plus tax)*

*U. S. PAT. #2830602

Max Factor, circa 1958.

Cova Loosprest

COMPACT **2**⁷⁵

plus 15¢ Fed. Tax

If she likes her powder spill-proof, give this
slim, golden COVA with a pattie of "Air Spun"
Loosprest Powder in L'ORIGAN fragrance.

For loose powder fans, the same vanity costs only 2.00. No Fed. Tax

Coty "Cova Loosprest" compact, circa 1951.

Cosmetic houses, besides the actual compact manufacturers, began producing compact cases to hold their own cosmetics. Revlon, Yardley, Elizabeth Arden, Helena Rubinstein, Evening in Paris (Bourjois), Tangee, Djer-Kiss, Houbigant, Guerlain, Kathleen Mary Quinlan, Coty, Roger & Gallet, Max Factor, Harriet Hubbard Ayer, Woodbury's and Richard Hudnut were a few of the most well known. Natalie Thurston, a notable beauty consultant in the 1920s, also began designing her own line of compacts which were offered for sale in 1928 through the National Bellas Hess Company. The consumer was able to pick out the desired shade of powder or rouge and it was conveniently packaged in the decorative compact of her choice. By the 1930s, dozens of respectable beauty consultants began doing the very same thing and catalogues were full of beauty preparations available in metal compact and lipstick cases. For a brief period in the early forties, however, some cosmetic companies switched to plastic and cardboard packaging for their cosmetics due to war restrictions on certain metals.

Four piece "Evening in Paris" set consisting of cologne, talcum powder, powder compact and lipstick tube.

Brushed gold compact with raised bow design on lid, marked Goubaud de Paris; Gold-plated compact with engraved and enameled playing card motifs on lid, marked Wadsworth; Brushed goldtone compact with man leaning against a street lamp, unmarked.

Silver-plated double vanity compact with embossed nymphs on lid. The inside reveals powder sifter and rouge compartment, marked "Djer—Kiss Pat'd. 5-19-25."

Natalie Thurston double compact advertised in the National Bellas Hess catalogue, 1928.

Vanity cases and matching lipstick by Helena Rubinstein, *Vogue*, July, 1937.

Ivory compact and matching lipstick by Kathleen Mary Quinlan, *Vogue*, July, 1937.

Seven lipvues decorated with imitation pearls, imitation stones, mother-of-pearl and leather.

Solid perfume compact with hand painted porcelain top, marked Mary Chess, London, New York, Montreal.

Silver-plated purse mirror, embossed top with paper portrait under clear plastic panel; Round mirror made of brass with embossed rose design.

The glamourous styles created by the stars of the screen were constantly dictating the fashion of the period. Hollywood starlets helped promote the use of cosmetics as they were seen taking their compacts out of their purse, both on and off the screen, and powdering their noses. Compacts acted as props in old movies; a woman in a crowded room would take her compact out of her purse and use the mirror to locate that certain someone who might have been following her. The romance of a gentleman giving that special compact to that special lady was evidenced in movies as well as in numerous magazine advertisements. For over a half of a century, the vanity case or compact was an indispensable accessory that every woman possessed. Manufacturers continually stressed that this accessory should coordinate with a particular purse or even a particular dress thus promoting one compact for every outfit. In all probability, for extremely fashion conscious women, this was just the case.

Elgin American hand engraved "Mother" compact; round gold-plated double vanity decorated with mirrors on both sides, marked Elgin American.

Top—Goldtone and enamel compact, Eastern influence, marked Rex, Fifth Avenue. Bottom—Square goldtone compact with embossed designs further accented with green enamel by Dorset, Fifth Avenue.

Two goldtone compacts embellished with rhinestones by K & K (Kotler and Kopit).

Large celluloid compact with floral transfer on lid, marked Rex Fifth Avenue, circa 1939-40.

Genuine snakeskin lipvue and goldtone compact and lipstick tube fitted in genuine snakeskin carrying case.

Five jeweled folding purse combs.

Brushed goldtone lipvue and folding comb with engraved leaf, marked Marhill, Fifth Avenue.

Novelty fashion accessories including sewing kits and stamp boxes by Schildkraut.

Seven different examples of folding pocket or purse photo frames.

Open view of pocket photo frames that were extremely popular in the 1950s.

Matched set consisting of atomizer, powder jar, powder compact, rouge compact and lipstick tube made of blue plastic and electroplated base metal.

An inexpensive version of the *minaudière* was introduced in the 1930s and became known as the carryall. Certain examples were designed as large rectangular vanity cases fitted with compartments for powder, rouge, lipstick, cigarettes and lighter. Mirrors, combs and money holders were also included. These rectangular cases, usually goldtone metal (sometimes referred to as jeweler's bronze), were able to fit snugly into satin, suede, moire, faille or brocade carrying cases. Other versions were fashioned with a chain handle or a woven mesh strap attached directly to the case itself. Silver and goldtone varieties were extremely popular in addition to those made of mother-of-pearl, speckled Lucite, metal mesh, suede and leather. By the 1950s, carryalls had reached their peak in popularity.

Carryall and compacts by Volupté and Ansico made of genuine mother-of-pearl.

Large Lucite carryall with mesh strap handle. The Lucite is speckled with flakes of mother-of-pearl and further ornamented with blue glass stones.

Brocade carryall with mesh strap handle fitted with powder compartment, lipstick tube, coin purse and hair comb, marked Zell.

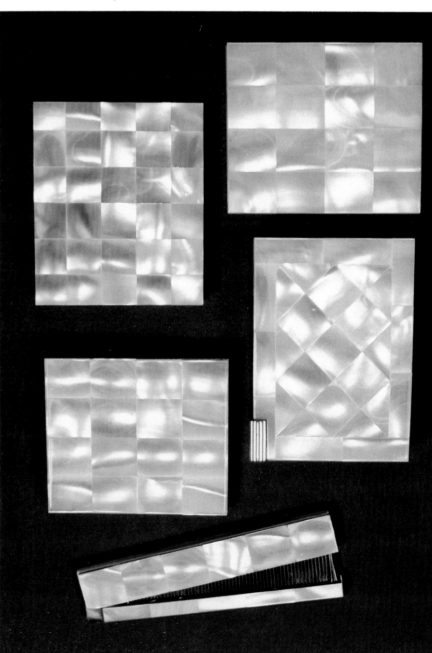

Mother-of-pearl carryall framed with rhinestones, lipstick attached on one side, marked Ansico, Genuine Mother-of-pearl; Silver- and gold-plated floral engraved carryall.

Goldtone carryall fitted with compartment for cigarettes, powder and mirror. The lipstick is attached to outside of case; Blue speckled Lucite carryall, marked Curry Arts; Mother-of-pearl carryall with lipstick and perfume attached to outside of case, marked Ansico.

Black speckled Lucite carryall by Zell, Fifth Avenue.

Zell Lucite carryall, shown open.

Matched set consisting of carryall, cosmetic clutch, cigarette case, photo frame, pillbox, purse comb and lipvue made of gold colored metal mesh, unmarked.

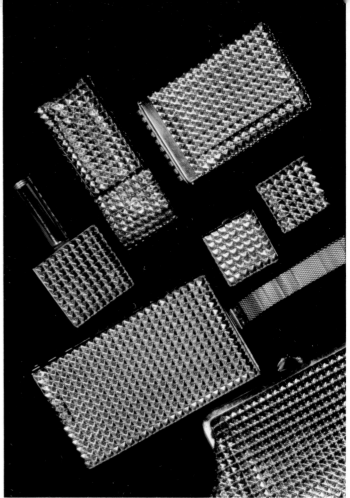

Yellow speckled Lucite carryall with snake chain handle; Large silver and gold speckled Lucite carryall with mesh strap handle by Curry Arts, Scranton, Pa.

Carryalls decorated with square tiles of genuine mother-of-pearl and rhinestones, marked Made in USA.

Two mother-of-pearl carryalls made by Ansico; Goldtone carryall decorated with hand painted cigarette and attached lipstick tube on side.

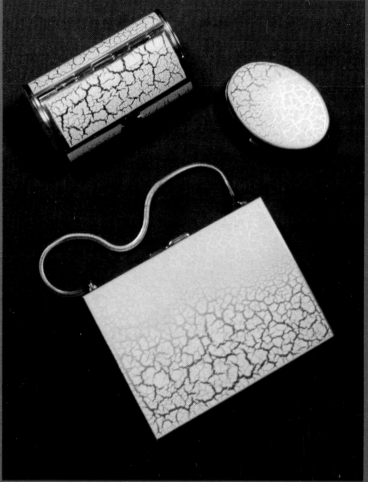

Matched set consisting of cigarette case, oval compact and carryall made of a gold plated base metal further decorated with enamel made with a crackled appearance, unmarked.

Gold confetti decorates this Lucite carryall by Wiesner of Miami.

Evans Deluxe Carryall featured in the Lee-Robert catalogue in 1950.

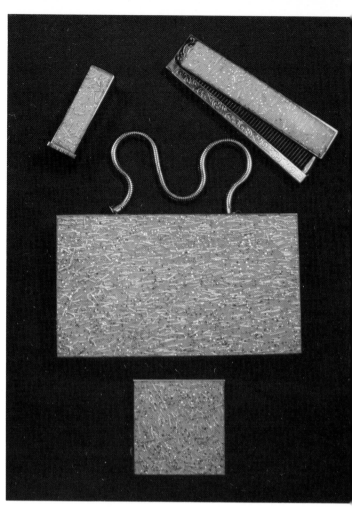

Pink speckled Lucite square compact, carryall, purse comb and lipstick by Curry Arts.

Evans

THE FINEST LIFETIME
Gift for a Lady
EVANS Deluxe CARRYALL

Evans carryall with flexible mesh handle in new basket weave design, golden metal finish. Contains lipstick, velour puff, powder well, lucite comb, coin holder and separate space for 14 cigarettes.
No. 17-180M1590................Retail Price $26.50*

An Evans deluxe carryall was offered in 1950 from the Lee-Robert Company of Chicago. It was designed in the basket weave pattern and held a powder well, puff, lipstick, Lucite comb, coin holder and a compartment for fourteen cigarettes. It retailed for $26.50. In 1953, Volupté offered their *Queen Lace Carryall* which was a royal blue and rhinestone studded vanity with fitted carrying case. This model sold for $30.00. These carryalls were never inexpensive, even when they were first introduced.

Vanity clutch bags were small envelope-style purses fitted with a separate compact, lipstick tube, perfume vial, hair comb and small mirror. These bags were popular from the late thirties to the fifties. Many were designed by Elizabeth Arden and Helena Rubinstein in the late thirties. A slightly larger vanity purse was manufactured with a powder compact which was mounted directly into the purse itself, usually at the top. This particular design allowed plenty of extra space beneath the compact for carrying other personal belongings. This style became the rage in the late forties. Bolster and hatbox-shaped vanity purses were fashionable in the fifties made of suede, faille, damask or brocade. Lin-Bren was a top manufacturer of vanity cluth bags and vanity purses.

A Volupté leather carryall called "Porte-Manteau", circa 1936.

"PORTE-MANTEAU" in Harlem tan diced calf . . . first appearance of the carry-all case in a tailored leather. *Shown in important stores.* Volupté, 347 Fifth Avenue, New York

Tailleur by **BONWIT TELLER**

"TIME ON YOUR HANDS," Watchcase compact. Clock face motif on white background. About $5.

"DÉSIRÉE," Compact, Inspired by the Literary Guild Selection, Désirée, published by Wm. Morrow & Co. Silver color with rhinestone crown. About $7.50*

"QUEEN'S LACE" Carryall. Rhinestone lace effect on royal blue background. About $30.*

"MORNING GLORY," Watchcase compact. Rhinestone floral design on white background. About $7.50*

Other lovely Volupté gifts from $2.00. At fine stores everywhere. Or write for the store nearest you.

deral Tax

VOLUPTÉ
reflects the prettiest faces!

OMPACTS • CIGARETTE CASES • CARRYALLS • LIGHTERS • PILLBOXES
347 Fifth Avenue, New York 16, New York

Volupté compacts and carryalls, circa 1953.

Mini-carryalls made of speckled Lucite by Curry Arts.

Brocade vanity clutch fitted with compact, lipstick tube, perfume vial and comb, unmarked.

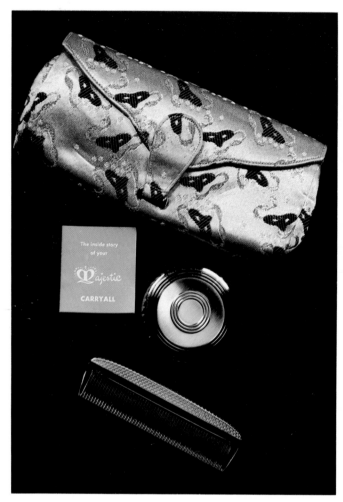

Fabric vanity clutch bag fitted with goldtone metal compact and Lucite comb, marked Majestic, Fifth Avenue.

Two brocade vanity clutch bags.

Vanity clutch and compact by Lin-Bren Products Corporation made of Koroseal, circa 1949.

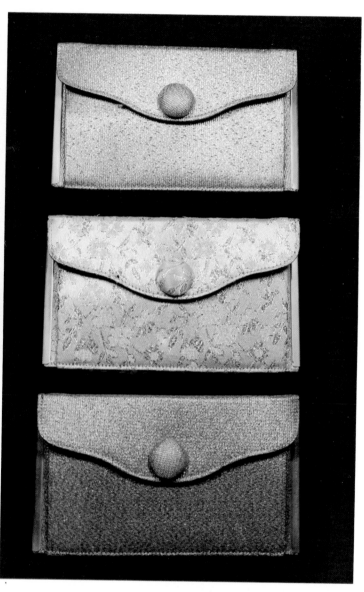

Three fabric vanity clutch bags by Lin-Bren. The bags are fitted wtih matching cloth-covered compacts.

Black and gold floral vanity clutch fitted with matching compact and Lucite comb, marked Lin-Bren.

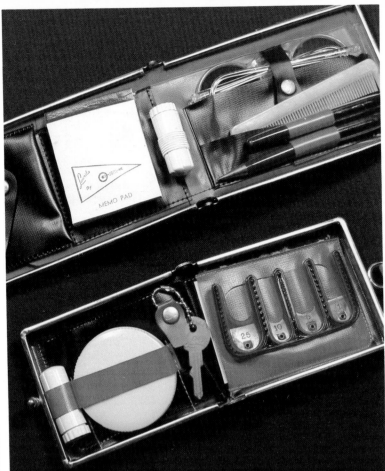

Inside view of plastic carryalls with novelty fittings geared for teenagers in the 1950s.

Four plastic novelty carryalls, marked Laurita.

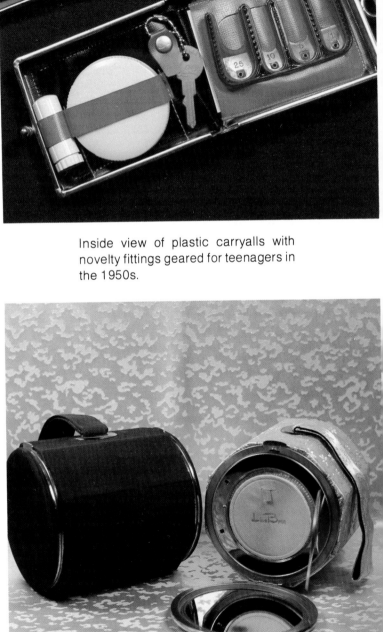

Octagonal-shaped vanity purses with wrist strap; one end opens to reveal a large powder compact and the opposite end has substantial area for housing other items. These vanity purses were made by Lin-Bren.

Vanity purse made of white brocade fitted with Lucite comb and matching compact, marked Lin-Bren, circa 1947-48.

Chocolate brown grosgrain vanity clutch fitted with Lucite comb and matching compact by Lin-Bren.

Two brown grosgrain vanity purses with plastic tops and matching compacts, marked Lin-Bren.

Two cloth-covered cylindrical vanity purses with matching cloth-covered powder compacts, marked Lin-Bren.

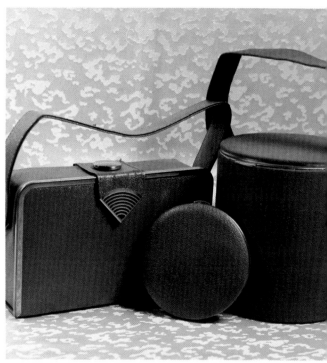

Green carryall fitted with comb, lipstick, matching powder compact and compartment for money and cigarettes, marked Lin-Bren, Pat. #2425540; Cylinder or bolster-shaped vanity purse made of green broadcloth and fitted with matching compact, marked Lin-Bren, circa 1947-48.

Two carryalls fitted with matching compacts, marked Lin-Bren, circa 1947-48.

Hundreds of manufacturing companies produced quality vanity cases, compacts, carryalls, mesh vanity bags, vanity clutches and vanity purses from the turn of the century until the 1960s. Most of the higher quality compacts were stamped with the manufacturers name either on the back of the compact, on the lid of the powder compartment, on the bottom of the powder well or on the powder puff. Other manufacturers used paper or transparent labels with the manufacturers name and they were usually attached to the mirror inside of the compact. If the compact was used to any degree, the label was probably removed before use. Occasionally, one is lucky enough to acquire a compact still in its original pouch and presentation box. Since many of these little treasures were given as gifts, finding examples in mint condition is possible. Some manufacturers, however, did not include any stampings or labels. This is usually common on insignificant mass produced examples. Other manufacturers put their marks on the cloth pouches and on the original presentation boxes that the compacts came in. Often, these clues to identification have been discarded.

Petty cash novelty compact popular in 1958.

Five genuine cowhide compacts made by Rumpps. The matching compact and pillbox on bottom left is marked Majestic.

A variety of novelty accessories "Styled by the Bucklers, Fifth Avenue, NY."

Wonderful display of jeweled lipstick holders by Ernest Steiner Inc., NY.

Novelty lipstick holders by Ernest Steiner Inc., NY.

Some of the most popular compact manufacturing companies were American Beauty, Curry Arts, Dorset, Elgin American, Evans, K&K, Kigu, Majestic, Marhill, Rex of Fifth Avenue, Schildkraut, Stratton of London, Volupté, Wadsworth, Wiesner of Miami, and Zell of Fifth Avenue. Fine jewelry companies like Asprey, Boucheron, Cartier, Fabergé, Tiffany and Van Cleef and Arpels also produced fine examples that are sought after today. Costume jewelry companies like Carnegie, Coro, Dior, Eisenberg and Givenchy produced fine examples that were sold in leading department stores. The Whiting and Davis Company, noted for fine mesh handbags and jewelry, also produced wonderful compacts, vanity bags and purse accessories. One of the most popular vanity bags made by Whiting and Davis was *The Delysia* which was in vogue in the 1920s. This firm is still in business today producing mesh handbags and fashion accessories. Well-known fashion designers created spectacular compacts for specific top of the line manufacturers. Elsa Schiaparelli designed fabulous compacts in the 1930s which were sold in leading department stores and boutiques. Spanish surrealist painter, Salvador Dali designed the "Bird-In-Hand" compact for Elgin American in 1950. This particular compact was available in three unique finishes and three different price ranges appealing to a large spectrum of buyers. This compact is extremely desirable today.

Two pocket picture frames with enameled lids and hand painted animal designs in center medallion, marked "Old Vienna", Styled by Schildkraut.

Compact and matching cigarette case by J.V.Pilcher Manufacturing Company, Louisville, Kentucky, circa 1948.

Lip-Vue by Schildkraut, circa 1947.

Compacts and cigarette cases by Rex
Fifth Avenue, circa 1947.

Genuine tortoiseshell compact by
Schildkraut; Brushed gold and hand
engraved compact by Marhill; Tiny
square compact with scenic transfer
on porcelain top.

Green Bakelite compact with gold-
plated hand engraved decorative strip
by Marhill. (Matching accessories
found on page 126.)

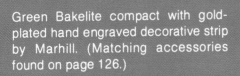

Goldtone compacts and pillboxes with rhinestone studded Bakelite tops.

Top—Two oval compacts decorated with rhinestones and enamel made by K&K (Kotler & Kopit, Inc.). Bottom— Oval goldtone compact ornamented with marcasite bow made in England by Kigu.

Heart-shaped solid perfume compact studded with pink rhinestones by Schiaparelli.

Round compact, square pill box and matching cigarette lighter, hand engraved and enameled, marked Marhill, Fashioned on Fifth Avenue, New York.

Oval butterfly compacts, marked K&K (Kotler & Kopit, Inc., Pawtucket, Rhode Island); Two black enameled compacts with cloisonné enamel medallion on lid.

Three compacts decorated with imitation pearls, rhinestones and molded coral-colored plastic flowers by K&K.

Variety of genuine snakeskin fashion accessories by Majestic.

Silver compact by Elsa Schiaparelli featured on the cover of the *Delineator* in February of 1933.

By the mid-sixties, the use of makeup was beginning to dwindle when natural beauty was again stressed. Eye makeup became the most popular cosmetic of the period. Since powder and rouge (now termed blush) were fading out of the fashion picture, most compact manufacturers virtually went out of business. The giant cosmetic companies like Avon, Coty, Max Factor, Revlon and Yardley continued to manufacture compacts to hold their lines of cosmetics. Eventually, however, disposable plastic compact cases were sold and decorative metal and jeweled varieties became an item of the past.

Purses Accessories

8735J4075—Sterling Silver engine-turned cigarette case holds full pack of Regular size or eighteen King size cigarettes. Has plaque for engraving initials. Size: 3⅝ x 3¼" x ¾". **Sugg. Retail $54.00**

8741J2250—Sterling Silver compact with inner-door powder compartment and clear glass mirror. Suitable for engraving. Size: 2¾" square. **Sugg. Retail $30.00**

A fine imported hand beaded bag and accessories. Gleaming Black beaded envelope bag and matching, beaded mirror-lipstick combination and beaded compact with inner door powder compartment.

	Sugg. Retail
8776J945—Black Beaded Bag	$14.00
8777J430—Beaded Compact (2½ x 2¼ x ½")	6.00
8778J288—Beaded Mirror-Lipstick Combination	4.00

Mother of Pearl Accessories

Lustrous genuine Oriental Mother of Pearl squares on jewelers bronze cases. A perennial favorite of unmatched beauty. The wafer-thin styling lends its appeal to every woman. Each item individually boxed.

	Sugg. Retail
(A) 8333J517—Cigarette Case (3¾"x3")	$7.00
(B) 8332J367—Compact (2¾"x2¼")	5.00
(C) 8740J235—Contact Lens Case (2"x1¼")	3.25
(A) 8790J400—Full-pak cigarette case (not shown)	6.00

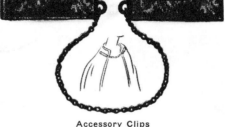

Accessory Clips

8647J360—Gold-tone clips for your sweater, jacket, scarf, or stole. Genuine hand-made petit point (1650 stitches to the square inch). **Sugg. Retail $5.00**

Petit-Point Compact

8058J1080—Genuine hand-made petit-point (1650 stitches to the square inch). Jewelers bronze metal lacquered and tarnish proof. Inner-door powder compartment, puff and clear glass mirror. Size: 2¾"x2⅜". **Sugg. Retail $15.00**

Purse accessories featured in the Bennett Brothers Blue Book in 1966.

It has only been in the last few years that serious attention has been given to collecting compacts and vanity cases. Much information is still waiting to be uncovered. A giant step, however, was taken by Roselyn Gerson with her wonderful and informative book, *Ladies' Compacts of the Nineteenth and Twentieth Centuries.* Because of the recent attention paid to this wonderful hobby, prices of vintage examples are rising. In addition, many leading companies from the past have started to manufacture these fun fashion accessories again. Leading jewelers, like Tiffany and Company, reintroduced some of their own "retro" compacts from the thirties, forties and fifties. Stratton of London is continually marketing new and different compacts and purse accessories. Contemporary cosmetic firms, like Estée Lauder, Yves Saint Laurent and Clinique also sell decorative compacts in conjunction with their specific cosmetic lines. Although these compacts are lovely, the originals offer a nostalgic charm associated with the romance of days gone by.

Imitation mother-of-pearl compact accented with goldtone medallion in center, marked Estée Lauder.

Three fan-shaped lipvues and folding comb, made in England by Stratton.

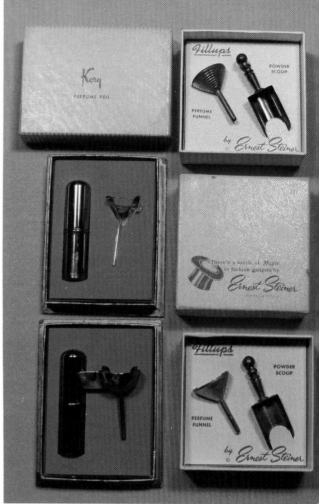

Powder scoop and perfume funnel by Ernest Steiner; Perfume vials and funnels by Kory Cosmetics, Inc.

Black enameled and lacquered convertible compact with scalloped edges and hand painted flowers on lid, designed to hold solid or loose powder, marked Stratton, Made in England.

Goldtone compact with oriental theme accompanied by original black felt pouch, marked Stratton, Made in England; Silvertone and enamel compact with engine-turned designs, marked Stratton.

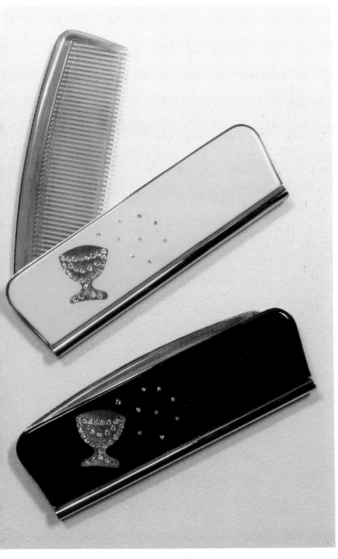

Two enameled purse combs studded with rhinestones in champagne glass motif made by Zell.

Novelty fashion accessories to include: "Gum Smoke", a combination gum and cigarette case; "Rain 'N Shine" which includes folding plastic sunglasses and a rain bonnet; "After Every Meal..." which includes a toothbrush and toothpaste; and finally "Have Gum...Will Travel" which is a case specifically designed to carry a full pack of gum. Also included is a traveling shaving kit, a first aid kit and a zipper pull.

Compact, pill box, picture holder, lipstick tube and perfume vial made of goldtone metal with cloisonné ornaments by Roth & Steiner Inc., New York.

Genuine dyed snakeskin fashion
accessories to include wallet, cigarette
cases, compacts, sewing kit, perfume
vial, key chain, manicure kit and photo
wallet by Alfred Dunhill.

Chapter III: Smoking Accessories

The use of tobacco in history

The practice of smoking tobacco has existed for many centuries. Initially cultivated by the American Indians, tobacco was believed to be sacred and was used in ceremonies and rituals. Soon the custom had become so sacred that it was believed to cure ailments and prevent certain contagious diseases. With the discovery of America in 1492, the crew of Columbus began enjoying the Indian ritual of smoking shredded tobacco leaves in pipes.

This Gay Nineties' cigar box label reveals the beginnings of women's emancipation and the desire to smoke in public.

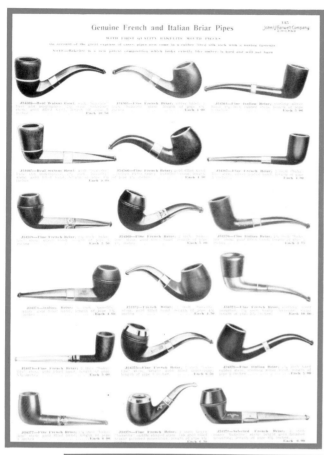

J34347—The Wilmort Ash Tray with Pipe Cleaning Attachment; solid brass mahogany finish; an ash tray that will be popular especially with a pipe smoker; has a pointed prong in center on which the pipe can be scraped out; bright nickel plated fittings and 5 inch removable glass lining.....**Each 5.00**

Circa 1920.

Genuine French and Italian Briar pipes with Bakelite stems, circa 1920.

Smoker's novelties offered for sale, circa 1900.

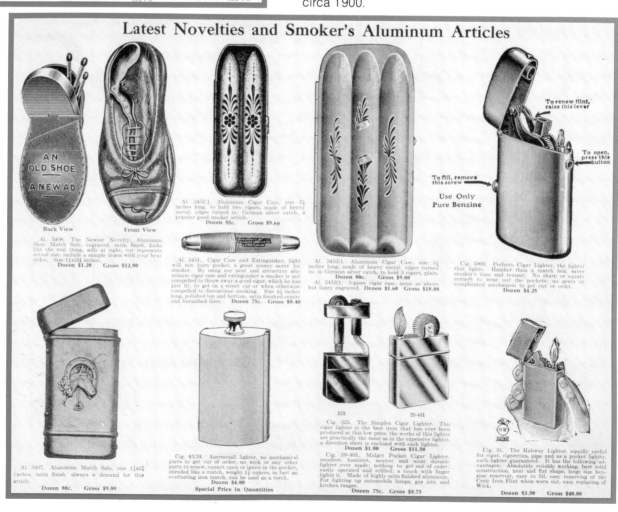

Tobacco was then cultivated in the West Indies in the early 1500s, spreading to Spain, then France in 1559, England in 1585 by Sir Francis Drake and finally to all of Europe. Various means of using tobacco became fashionable. For instance, the tobacco leaves would be rolled into cigars; the leaves would be shredded for pipes and later cigarettes; it could be processed for chewing; and finally ground into snuff. The wealthy Spaniards preferred smoking cigars while the wealthy Englishmen preferred pipe smoking which was introduced by Sir Walter Raleigh. By the early seventeenth century, the use of tobacco in one form or another had reached all corners of the globe.

In the middle of the seventeenth century, snuff was considered "chic" and gorgeous snuff boxes made of solid gold with enamel ornamentation were commissioned by wealthy noblemen. Less expensive snuff boxes were made of wood, tortoiseshell, horn and pewter.

When the wealthy Spaniards discarded their cigar butts, the street beggars would gather them up and roll the remaining tobacco shreds in scraps of paper. This newest version of a tobacco product was later to be known as cigarettes. Originally called *papeletes* or *cigarillos*, these so-called "poor man's smokes" became common practice for wealthy and poor alike by the late eighteenth century. During the Napoleonic wars, the French troops were introduced to these little cigars and they were then renamed cigarettes. During the Civil War, American soldiers enjoyed smoking cigarettes with a fondness for blended tobacco, especially Turkish and American.

By 1880 in America, James A. Bonsack was issued a patent for a cigarette machine. Three years later, this invention was available in England. By 1895, small cigarette making machines, designed for personal use, were sold through mail-order catalogues retailing for twenty-five cents. From that time on, cigarette smoking became fashionable, especially for the male gender. It was not until World War I with women's emancipation, that smoking taboos were finally lifted for women so they could enjoy the freedom of smoking in public. It did not have to be a secret anymore

Accessories for smokers

Increased popularity of smoking tobacco prompted manufacturers to produce elegant smoking accessories for the pocket and the purse. Until this point, however, pipes, tobacco cases, snuff boxes and match safes had most often been elaborately made in expensive materials. Throughout the nineteenth century, however, women filled their leisure time with handwork in one form or another. Cigar cases were often made of Berlin Wool Work and tobacco pouches were crocheted of silk and given as

This engraved match safe sold for $5.25 in 1895.

Sterling silver match safe made in the Art Nouveau style with repoussé work.

gifts to that special man. The Industrial Revolution, booming in the second half of the same century, allowed manufacturers to produce large quantities of smoking accessories in inexpensive materials to be sold at much lower prices. Large cigar cases and decorative match safes were mass produced in sterling silver, silver plate on a nickel base and nickel plate on a brass base. Aluminum as a lightweight metal was also popular. Engraved, embossed, chased, fluted, hammered and enameled designs were abundant.

Three elaborate match safes with repoussé work and all inscribed with monograms. *Her Own Place.*

Three match safes made of sterling silver. *Her Own Place.*

MATCH SAFE
(Cut actual size)
Solid Sterling silver, beautiful hammered design. Well made and finished.
No. 43H   Each........$7.60

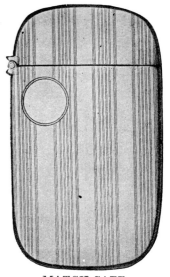

MATCH SAFE
(Cut actual size)
Highest grade silver plated rich engine turned design, plain back. Signet for engraving.
No. 042/08 Each.......$5.00

Match safes advertised for sale in 1923.

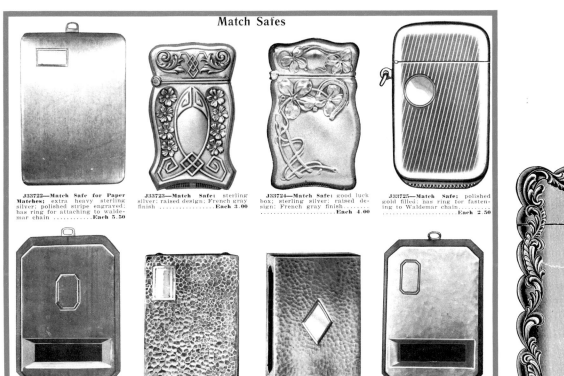

Match safes offered for sale from John
V. Farwell in 1920.

Match safe with Rococo border on
both sides, circa 1895.

Cigar and cigarette cases

Cigar cases were designed to hold one cigar or a half of a
dozen cigars. Novelty items included cigar cases that would hold
one cigar with an extinguisher built into the case. The purpose for
this novelty was so the smoker was "not compelled to throw away
a good cigar, which he had just lit, to get on a street car or when
otherwise compelled to discontinue smoking."

In 1895, cigar and smaller cigarette cases were offered from
the BHA Illustrated Catalogue in various leathers such as seal
and lizard with silk linings and embossed silver decorations. They
also offered cigarette cases made of quadruple plate on a nickel
silver base or oxidized on nickel silver. Other companies offered
embossed leather cases, made in the telescope style, to fit softly
into the pocket, yet protecting the cigars or cigarettes at the same
time.

Cigar and cigarette cases made of seal
and lizard skin, circa 1895.

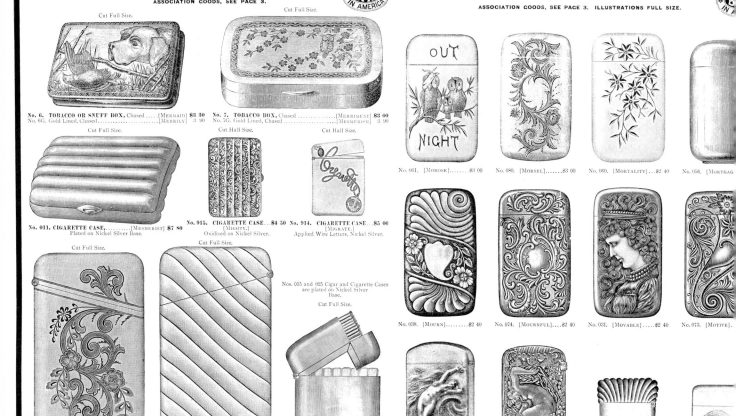

FINEST QUADRUPLE SILVER PLATED WARE.

ASSOCIATION GOODS, SEE PAGE 3.

Cut Full Size.

Cut Full Size.

No. 6. TOBACCO OR SNUFF BOX, Chased ..... [MERMAID] $3 30
No. 6G. Gold Lined, Chased .... [MERRILY] 3 90

No. 7. TOBACCO BOX, Chased .... [MERRIMENT] $3 00
No. 7G. Gold Lined, Chased .... [MESMERISM] 3 90

Cut Full Size.

Cut Half Size.

Cut Half Size.

No. 011. CIGARETTE CASE. .... [MESMERIST] $7 80
Plated on Nickel Silver Base.

No. 915. CIGARETTE CASE... $4 50
[MIGHTY.]
Oxidized on Nickel Silver.

No. 914. CIGARETTE CASE.. $5 00
[MIGRATE.]
Applied Wire Letters, Nickel Silver.

Cut Full Size.

Cut Full Size.

Nos. 015 and 025 Cigar and Cigarette Cases
are plated on Nickel Silver Base.

Cut Full Size.

No. 015. CIGAR CASE, Engraved .. $7 20
[MINARET.]
No. 015. Plain Satin ..... [MINATORY] 6 00

No. 015F. CIGAR CASE, Fluted.. [MINCE] $6 00

No. 025. CIGARETTE AND MATCH
CASE, Satin .... [MINCING] $6 00

71

FINEST QUADRUPLE SILVER PLATED WARE.

ASSOCIATION GOODS, SEE PAGE 3. ILLUSTRATIONS FULL SIZE.

No. 061. [MOROSE]...... $3 00

No. 080. [MORSEL]...... $3 00

No. 060. [MORTALITY]... $2 40

No. 056. [MORTGAG

No. 038. [MOURN]........ $2 40

No. 074. [MOURNFUL]... $2 40

No. 031. [MOVABLE]..... $2 40

No. 073. [MOTIVE]

No. 1. [MOWING] $2 50

No. 2. [MUFFLE] $2 50

No. 075. [MULLING]..... $2 10

No. 045. [MULTIFOR

Smoking accessories popular in 1895.

Silver-plated match safes popular in 1895.

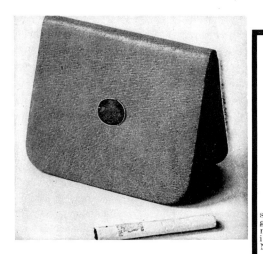

Pig skin moire-lined cigarette case (holds full pack) with solid gold monogram shield. This case cost $12.00 in 1918.

**SOLID SILVER
MATCH SAFE**
Rich engine turned design with space for engraving. (Holds paper matches). Length, 2½ inches.
No. 40/213   Each.... $7.15

**SOLID SILVER
MATCH SAFE**
(Cut reduced size)
Rich engine turned design with space for engraving. (Holds paper matches). Length 2¼ inches.
No. 57/201   Each.... $8.00

**SOLID SILVER
MATCH SAFE**
(Cut reduced size)
Magnificent hammered design with shield for engraving. (Holds paper matches). Length 2½ inches.
No. 66H   Each..... $9.2

Match safes designed to hold cardboard or paper matches were also called Match Book Cases.

Match safes

Match safes, which held wooden matches, were made in abundance with many styles to choose from. Very ornate sterling silver match safes were extremely common in addition to those made of German silver, silveroin, gunmetal, nickel, aluminum, gilt, nickel- and silver-plate. Engraved, embossed and repoussé designs were prevalent. Combination match safes and cigar cutters were made in abundance.

Lighters

By 1900, lighters became stylish and match safes began to lose some of their favor, although they were still offered for sale until the 1920s. The modern smoker, however, preferred a lighter in his pocket. Lighters were advertised as "handier than a match box." Manufacturers also stressed that lighters save "the smoker's time and temper." They were made with rounded corners so as not to wear out the pockets of men's clothing. Lighters were made to be easily refilled and used for many other purposes besides lighting pipes, cigars and cigarettes. For example, they were designed to light gas jets, kitchen stoves and automobile lamps. Match book cases also became common in the early twentieth century. Instead of holding wooden matches as did the match safe, the match book case was a decorative accessory used to hold cardboard matches.

Pocket watch-shaped lighter, circa 1913.

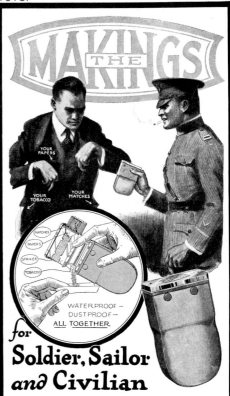

The "Makings" combination case designed to hold tobacco, papers and matches for making your own cigarettes, *Harper's Bazaar*, December 1918.

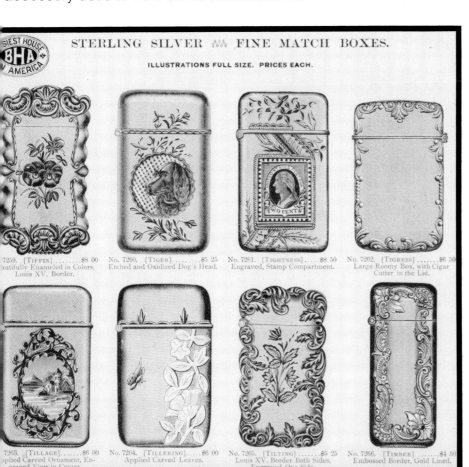

Sterling silver match boxes, circa 1895.

Jewelry stores

With the increased popularity for smoking and its accessories, fine jewelry stores began carrying smoking accessories as "standard jewelry store items." By the 1920s, a survey was conducted among jewelry store owners to find out if they would carry cigar and cigarette lighters as standard inventory. Nine out of ten jewelers who participated said that they would carry lighters at all times. Further findings concluded that twenty-four out of twenty-five pocket lighters that were sold were bought as gift items. The majority of the customers were women buying the lighters for men.

Men's leather smoking accessories, circa 1935.

Four hand-carved genuine ivory cigarette holders made in China.

Cigar and cigarette holders

Cigar and cigarette holders were extremely fashionable in the early twentieth century, particularly stylish in the Roaring Twenties. Choice materials were genuine ivory, briar, horn and meerschaum, ornamentally carved, with 14K gold, gold-filled or rolled gold plated mountings. Amber was also used extensively. When Bakelite became popular, fancy cigar and cigarette holders were made of this new composition which was very durable and reminiscent of amber. Bakelite does not burn, making it a likely candidate for cigar and cigarette holders. In 1902, Sears, Roebuck & Co. offered twisted rubber cigar holders which were designed to "give a nice cool smoke." Smokers' sundries were advertised and sold everywhere. In 1920, the John V. Farwell Company offered Bakelite cigar and cigarette holders with decorative silver and polished gold-filled mountings. Prices ranged from $2.75 to $5.00 and each holder came in a silk pocket case. In the same year, the I. Scheuer Company sold Bakelite holders with rolled gold mountings for as low as $1.00 each accompanied by a suede pocket case. Ivory cigarette holders of different lengths with 14K gold mountings were also available from this company, ranging in price from $2.50 to $7.50. Each holder came in a silk moire pocket (a leather case with chamois lining cost $1.00 extra).

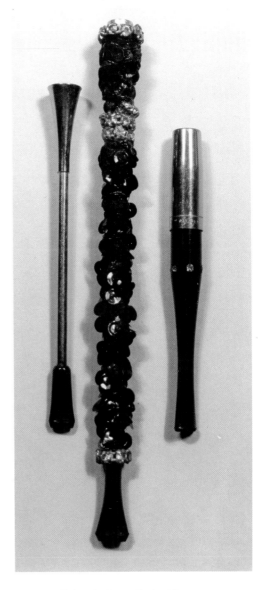

Trio of cigarette holders.

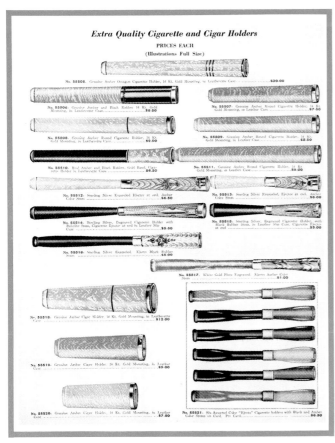

Cigar and cigarette holders, circa 1935.

Bakelite cigar and cigarette holders featured in the John V. Farwell catalogue, circa 1920.

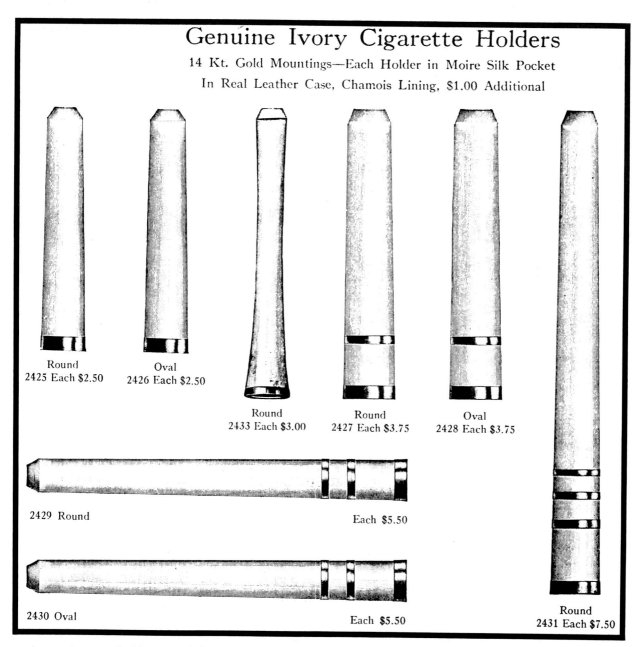

Genuine Ivory Cigarette Holders
14 Kt. Gold Mountings—Each Holder in Moire Silk Pocket
In Real Leather Case, Chamois Lining, $1.00 Additional

Round
2425 Each $2.50

Oval
2426 Each $2.50

Round
2433 Each $3.00

Round
2427 Each $3.75

Oval
2428 Each $3.75

2429 Round

Each $5.50

2430 Oval

Each $5.50

Round
2431 Each $7.50

Ivory cigarette holders, the I. Scheuer
Co., New York City, circa 1920.

Bakelite cigarette holder in original
presentation box.

Hand-carved cigarette holder, marked
"Warranted Genuine Meershaum" (also
spelled Meerschaum).

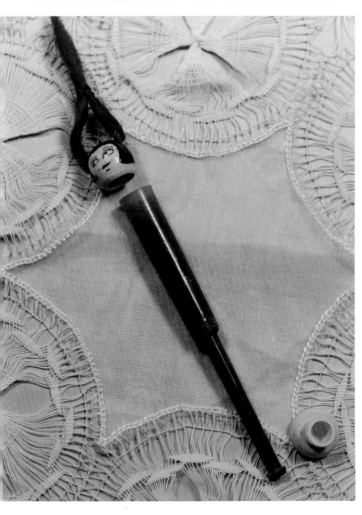

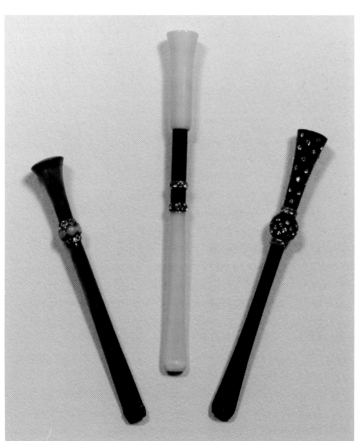

Novelty cigarette holder made of Bakelite shown open.

Novelty cigarette holder made of Bakelite, shown closed.

Three rhinestone studded Bakelite cigarette holders.

Two sterling silver and Bakelite cigarette holders, marked Napier; Two red plastic cigarette holders trimmed in silver by Dunhill.

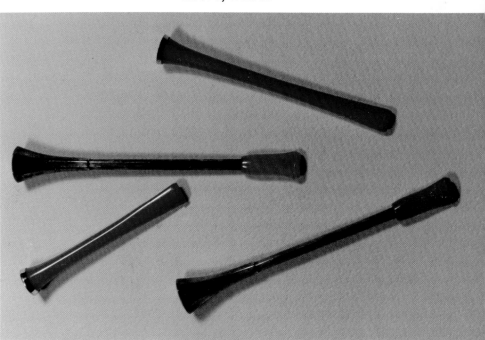

Embossed German silver cigarette case, marked E P Co. *Christine Ketchel.*

Men's cases

By the second decade of the twentieth century, cigarette cases instinctively gained impetus as the preferable accessory for men, and as always, manufacturers catered to the whims of the buying public. Thin model cases were modish in hammered, engraved, embossed and engine-turned designs. Occasionally a combination of two different designs were executed on the same case. For example, an engine-turned design on a hammered background was common. Also offered were cases with shields for monograms. Most cigarette cases of this period had gold-lined damaskeened interiors and a spring lever for holding cigarettes in place. Rectangular and square cases held up to sixteen cigarettes while oblong cases held up to twenty two cigarettes. Women were also able to purchase cigarette cases but they were more delicately designed and frequently smaller than their counterparts for men.

Silver-plated cigarette case with wonderful embossed design of a woman, Art Nouveau style, circa 1900. *Her Own Place.*

Two slimline cigarette cases made of nickel silver decorated with engine-turned designs.

Slimline cigarette case made of sterling silver and inlaid 14K gold. *Her Own Place.*

Celluloid cigarette case made to resemble tortoiseshell with rhinestone ornamentation.

Slimline style cigarette case in original presentation box, marked Silver 950 Matsuya (Japanese process of incorporating different metals into one particular design). *Her Own Place.*

Sterling silver cigarette case with Oriental-style engraving, marked 950 Silver. *Her Own Place.*

Hand engraved sterling silver cigarette case inscribed "From LR to LJ 1923." *Her Own Place.*

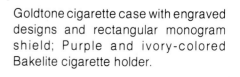

Goldtone cigarette case with engraved designs and rectangular monogram shield; Purple and ivory-colored Bakelite cigarette holder.

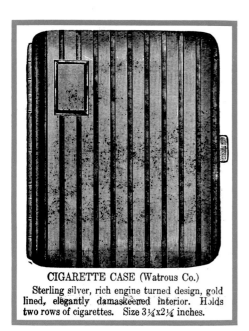

CIGARETTE CASE (Watrous Co.)
Sterling silver, rich engine turned design, gold lined, elegantly damaskeened interior. Holds two rows of cigarettes. Size 3¼x2¼ inches.

This sterling silver cigarette case was offered for $20.00 in 1923.

In 1919, The Elgin American Manufacturing Company offered cigarette cases in solid gold, gold-filled, sterling silver and nickel silver. The styles ranged from plain cases to those accented with engine-turned designs and enamel ornamentation. One particular case that was offered was called the "Elgin Cig-Photo Case." This case concealed a hidden compartment for holding two photographs along with the section designed for holding ten cigarettes. Another case offered for women was one with a card compartment attached to a chain handle. This company also designed cigarette cases for women with attached powder compacts.

In 1923, The Watrous Silver Company offered sterling silver cigarette cases accented with engine turned and hammered designs. The insides were gold-lined and large enough to hold two rows of cigarettes. Prices ranged from $18.50 for a sterling silver case with an engine-turned design on one side to $33.60 for a thin model case with a beveled edge, a 14K gold center stripe and a shield for a monogram. A silver-plated thin model case cost considerably less at $9.80.

Men's cigarette cases designed to hold from 11 to 22 cigarettes, circa 1935.

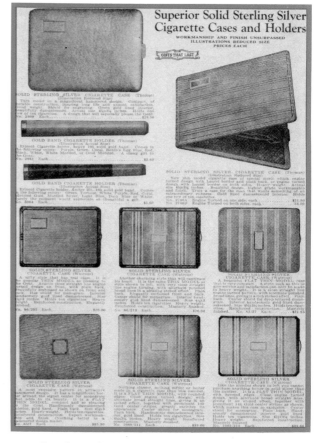

Sterling silver cigarette cases and Erinoid cigarette holders by Thomae and Watrous, circa 1923.

Sterling silver cigarette cases designed for men in 1935.

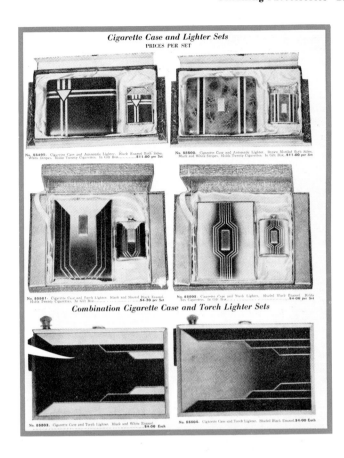

Cigarette case and lighter sets displaying modernistic designs, circa 1935.

Other novelties included the "Klever Kase" which was a cigarette case with a spring attachment that allowed the cigarette to practically pop out when the case was opened. The "Presto" case was another novelty, called presto because it could be opened with one hand. Two tabs, one at each side of the case, were pushed simultaneously allowing the top to spring open. It was a clever presentation when offering someone a cigarette.

The demand for cigarette cases grew dramatically in the thirties. As with compacts and vanities, prolific manufacturers produced cigarette cases made of many materials and designed in many styles appealing to men and women of all levels of income. In 1938, a novelty cigarette case was even advertised "For the young girl who's mad about horses..." This case, covered with calf fur and saddled with russet leather, was "large enough to hold a supply of cigarettes for all her friends." It sold for $10.00.

Three novelty cigarette cases with enameled and rhinestone studded cigarette motifs on the lids, circa 1950s.

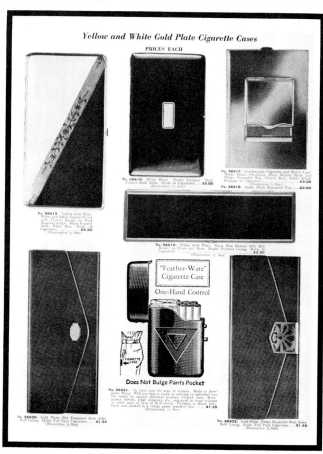

Benj. Allen & Co. offered these novelty cigarette cases in 1935.

Smoking accessories by Henry Lederer & Bro., Inc., *The Keystone*, September, 1929.

Goldtone cigarette case decorated with enameled animal motifs by Volupté.

Enameled cigarette cases with modernistic and novelty designs, circa 1935.

Engine-turned, embossed, chased and hammered cigarette cases offered in 1935.

Cigarette case and matching triple vanity case with flower basket motif, marked Langlois, Cara Nome, NY.

Two slimline pearl-topped cigarette cases made by Wiesner of Miami.

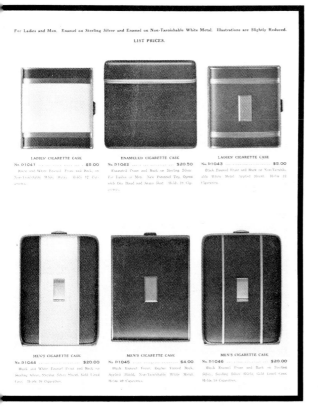

Enameled cigarette cases offered for sale from the H.M.Manheim Company in 1933.

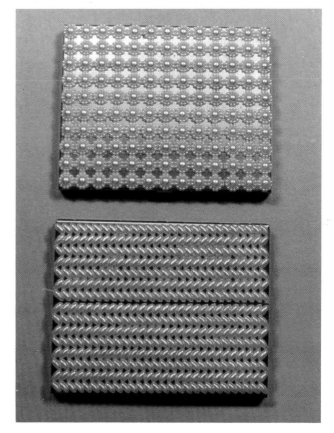

Oblong cigarette case, matching lighter and folding purse comb made of hand engraved gold electroplate and green marble-like Bakelite, marked Marhill. When the oblong cigarette case is opened, an attached goldtone lighter pops up on the inside.

Three gold-plated and enameled cigarette cases.

Volupté slimline combination cigarette case and lighter called the Volupté Lighter Case popular in the 1930s.

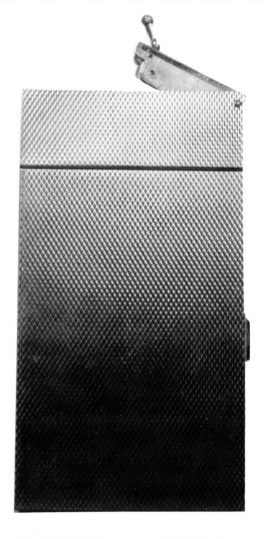

Gold mesh cigarette case with
rhinestone studded top.

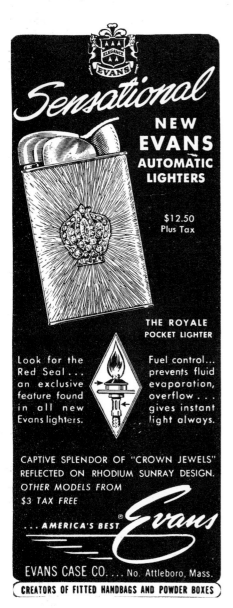

Evans Automatic cigarette lighter in rhodium sunray design, *Life*, 1949.

Manufacturers

The Evans Case Company also offered complete smoking sets, decorative table lighters, ash trays and humidors. Evans enameled sets, which were available in the late twenties, were excellent examples of the modernistic trends associated with the Art Deco and Art Moderne periods. Besides the striking geometrics rendered in enamel, Evans also employed various leathers to include pig skin, ostrich and alligator. Delicate cloisonné enamel work was also seen on items designed for women.

In 1929, Elgin manufactured its new "Watch Lighter" which was available in sterling silver and chromium plate. This popular item, made in a very thin model case, was a cigarette lighter and watch combination. It was designed so that all of the moving parts were concealed and it was described to "keep accurate time under the extreme difficulties imposed on such a timekeeper."

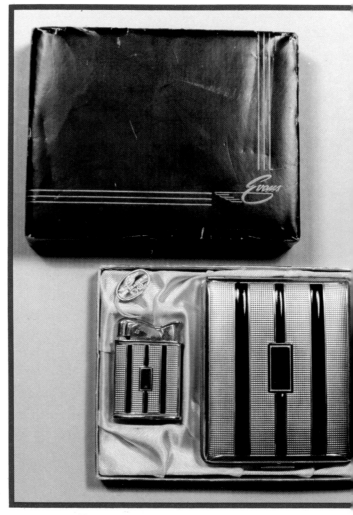

Evans chromium-plated and enameled cigarette case and matching lighter in original presentation box.

ELEGANT LIGHTERS Economy Priced

A **Evans Combination Cigarette Case and Lighter.** Handsome rhodium finish. Case holds 14 cigarettes . . . strong clasp keeps them secure. Built-in lighter on top is fully automatic . . . dependable. Size 4⅜x2½ inches.
87 D 4543—Postpaid (Shpg.wt.5 oz.) $3.95

B **Evans Standard.** Fully automatic lighter. Rhodium finish; engraving shield. Size 1½x2 inches.
87 D 4599—Postpaid (Shpg.wt.8 oz.) $2.95

Evans lighters are guaranteed for 1 year against defects in material or workmanship.

C **Cloisonne,** the perfect Evans lighter for a woman. Exquisitely styled . . gold-color metal set with a floral design cloisonne. Smartly boxed. Fully automatic. Size 2x1⅜-in.
87 D 4536—Postpaid (Wt. 4 oz.) $3.95

D **Evans Cosmopolitan.** This distinguished lighter gave 2,007 lights without refuelling in a Sears Laboratory test. Reduces failure due to fuel shortage. Fully automatic. Protective windguard. Rhodium finish. 2⅜x1⅜-in.
87 D 4568—Postpaid (Wt. 8 oz.).. $3.25

Evans lighters offered for sale from Sears, Roebuck & Company in 1953.

EVANS

EVANS
NEW ROLLER BEARING ACTION

Lighter Magic is achieved in the New Evans—the magic of modern mechanical perfection.

Cross Lever, Roller Bearing Action is a new principle in lighter building—exclusively Evans. It means smoother action, wider clearance between snuffer and wick, an almost complete revolution of the sparking wheel that spurts a veritable shower of sparks to insure ignition—not at one, but at several points in the revolution of the wheel, from just one pressure of the thumb. The removable wick holder is a unique convenience and all steel parts are specially hardened to assure long wear.

ITS STYLE NEVER FAILS TO REGISTER— ITS WICK NEVER FAILS TO LIGHT!

E1625—White finish basket weave design .... $6.00 ea.

E1626—White finish, genuine leather cover, lizard grain. $6.00 ea.

E1627—White finish in contrasting French enamel front, neutral initial monogram design. $7.50 ea.

E1628—White finish, engine turned design in modernistic pattern with hand painted French enamel decoration. $6.00 ea.

E1629—White finish, modernistic design, of French enamel, shark grain background. $7.50 ea.

E1630—White finish, modernistic design, French enamel front in contrasting colors. $7.50 ea.

E1631—White finish, engine turned design with French enamel in contrasting color effects. .... $7.50 ea.

E1632—White finish, shark grain effect with French enamel stripes in contrasting colors. $7.50 ea.

E1633—White finish, modernistic design, contrasting French enamel colors in shark grain effect background. $7.50 ea.

E1634—White finish, in all over French enamel effect in contrasting colors .... $7.50 ea.

E1635—White finish, genuine Viennese egg shell enamel front with contrasting genuine hand engraved decoration. $12.00 ea.

E1636—White finish, French enamel front in contrasting colors with egg shell design. $9.00 ea.

E1637—Green gold finish, genuine ostrich cover with shield. $9.00 ea.

E1638—White finish, genuine hand painted Dresden enamel front .... $12.00 ea.

Illustrations actual size.

The LINE with the STERLING TOUCH

Evans cigarette lighters featured in
The Keystone, September, 1929.

E1648—Combination paper weight and automatic Roller Bearing desk lighter in contrasting colors of French enamel, polished green finish.................. $7.50 ea.

E1649—The Alladin Lamp of Learning combination paper weight and automatic Roller Bearing desk lighter, antique green finish. $18.00 ea.

E1650—Combination paper weight and automatic Roller Bearing desk lighter, genuine ostrich covered, polished green finish...... $8.25 ea.

E1651—Automatic Roller Bearing desk or table lighter, genuine leather covered in Bombay reptile grain, polished green finish. $10.50 ea.

E1652—Desk or table combination with removable automatic Roller Bearing lighter unit and ash receptacle in French enamel, polished green finish....... $10.50 ea.

E1653—Automatic Roller Bearing desk or table lighter in contrasting colors of French enamel, polished green finish.............. $9.00 ea.

E1654—Automatic Roller Bearing desk or table lighter, contrasting colors of French enamel, polished green finish............ $9.00 ea.

E1655—Desk or table combination with removable automatic Roller Bearing lighter unit and ash receptacle in contrasting colors of French enamel, polished green finish................... $10.50 ea.

E1656—Automatic novelty desk or table lighter in contrasting colors of French enamel, removable top serving as ash tray...... $9.00 ea.

Illustrations two-third size.

The LINE with the STERLING TOUCH

Evans Table lighters featured in *The Keystone*, September, 1929.

Cigarette case and matching cigarette lighters embellished with multi-colored glass stones, marked Evans.

Trio of gold mesh cigarette cases with genuine mother-of-pearl and rhinestone tops made by Evans called "Evans Serv-Pac, Holds full Pack, a touch of the thumb opens case and automatically raises cigarette for service."

Cigarette Case and Lighter Sets by Evans featured in the Hagn's Holiday Gift Flyer, circa 1934.

Leather covered lighter and cigarette case featured in the Sears, Roebuck & Company catalogue, circa 1930.

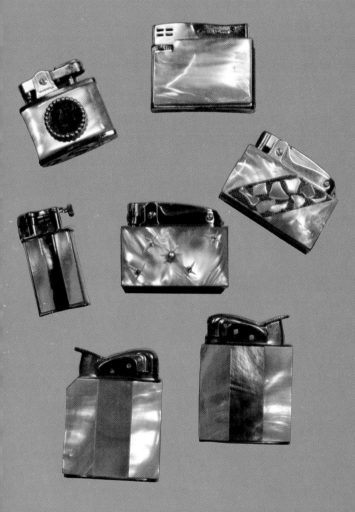

Six Lucite cigarette lighters by Evans Case Company, Attleboro, Massachusetts.

Genuine and imitation mother-of-pearl cigarette lighters. The genuine mother-of-pearl lighters were made by Evans; the imitations were fashioned by Marhill.

Cigarette lighter and matching comb decorated with rhinestones by Evans; Cigarette lighter and miniature compact enriched with rhinestones and molded plastic coral-colored flowers by Evans.

Six cigarette lighters decorated with cultured pearls, rhinestones, enamel and engraving by Evans and Marhill.

Variety of dyed cowhide cigarette lighters by Evans.

Trio of enameled and hand-painted cigarette lighters made by Evans.

Evans cigarette cases and matching
lighters popular in 1929 advertised in
The Keystone.

Evans Smoking Sets, *The Keystone*,
September, 1929.

Combination cigarette cases and lighters by Ronson and Evans, circa 1937.

Ladies' cigarette cases made of yellow and white gold plate enriched with enamel, circa 1935.

A delicately styled ladies' smoking set, circa 1927.

Yellow and White Gold Plate Ladies' Cigarette Cases

PRICES EACH
(Illustrations ¾ Size)

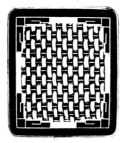

No. 56551. Yellow Gold Plate. Black Enamel Back. Fancy Combination Yellow Gold and Black Enamel Front. Engine Turned. Hold 14 Cigarettes....$4.00

No. 56552. Yellow Gold Plate. Black Enamel Back. Fancy Black and White Enamel Basket Weave Design Front. Holds 20 Cigarettes....$4.50

No. 56553. Yellow Gold Plate. Black Enamel Front and Back. Fancy Design with Silhouette on Top. Holds 14 Cigarettes....$3.70

No. 56554. White Metal, Chromium Plate. Black Enameled Both Sides. Modernistic Design on Front. Holds 14 Cigarettes....$3.70

No. 56555. Silver Plate, Black and White Enameled Front and Back, Gold Lined. Holds 6 Cigarettes....$3.00

No. 56556. White Gold Plate, Black Enameled Both Sides. Engine Turned Stripes. Holds 14 Cigarettes....$3.00

No. 56557. White Metal. Black Enamel Both Sides. Holds 12 Cigarettes....$2.80
No. 56558. Same, White Enameled....2.80

No. 56559. Brushed Gold Satin Finish Both Sides on White Metal. Rhinestone and Filigree Plaque on Top. Cedar Lined. Holds 12 Cigarettes....$2.00
No. 56560. Same, in Silver....2.00
No. 56561. Same, in Black....2.00
No. 56562. Same, in Red....2.00

No. 56562. White Gold Plate. Engine Turned Both Sides. Holds 14 Cigarettes....$2.80

Opposite page, bottom left:
Three Elgin American jeweled "Magic Action" cigarette lighters, covered with lacquer to prevent tarnishing accompanied by original pouch and box. These lighters originally sold for $13.50.

Opposite page, bottom right:
Three Elgin American cigarette lighters accented with hand-engraved fronts.

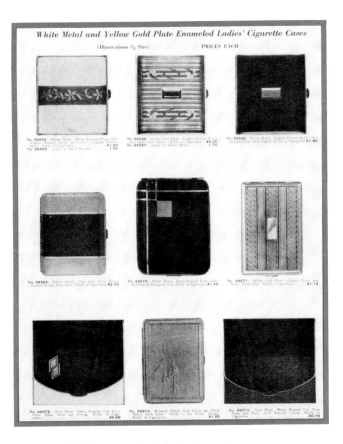

Variety of ladies' cigarette cases designed to hold from 6 to 16 cigarettes, circa 1935.

Three cigarette lighters covered with genuine snakeskin, alligator and ostrich leather, marked Elgin American Magic Action.

Swank Automatic Lighters were popular in the 1930s due to their reliable "sure-fire" light, slim design and ultra modern appearance. Enamel, mother of pearl and genuine leather models were stylish. They retailed from about $2.50 to $7.50 in 1933 with the mother of pearl model as the most expensive.

Swank Automatic Lighter Sets, circa 1933.

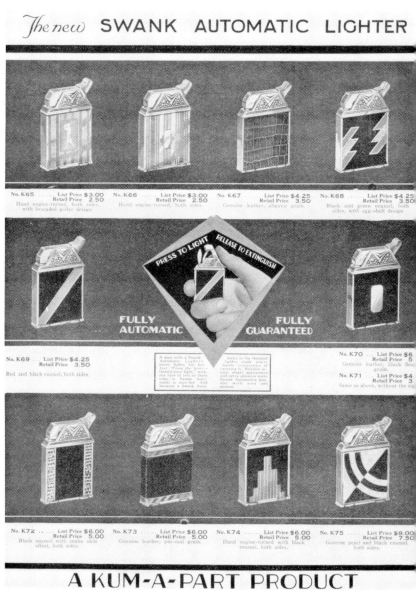

Swank Automatic cigarette lighters, H.M. Manheim, circa 1933.

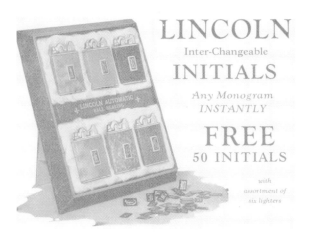

Lincoln inter-changeable initial lighters with nickel-silver bezels popular in 1929.

NEW! THE ONLY POCKET LIGHTER IN THE WORLD THAT GIVES YOU

6 MONTHS OF LIGHTS

WITHOUT REFUELING!*

No fooling with liquid fuels . . . No fiddling with wicks . . . Just a clean, clear, *hot* flame from cold *iso*-butane gas!

You've read about it—heard about it—now's your time to own a Parker Flaminaire! It's made by The Parker Pen Company, under the original French patents—the *only* pocket lighter in the world, regardless of fuel used, that gives you six months of safe, sure lights without refueling (*even if you smoke as much as a pack a day!). The Parker Flaminaire is fueled with clean, odorless, pure *iso*-butane. More than 300,000 users the world over are delighted with their Flaminaire lighters—and you'll be delighted, too, with its seemingly *everlasting* lighting ability. See it— at smart dealers everywhere.

Buy it now—for yourself, for a gift; it won't need refueling till next fall!

IN STUNNING GIFT CASE—$12.50
(NO F. E. TAX)

PARKER FLAMINAIRE

MADE BY THE PARKER PEN COMPANY, U. S. A.

Precision-made to the same high standards achieved in the Parker "51" Pen—the world's most-wanted pen.

©1951—The Parker Pen Company.

Parker "Flaminaire" precision lighter,
Life, 1951.

Left—Pencil Lighter made of chromium plate and red plastic, marked HAVALITE; Ronson Penciliter made of chromium plate and plastic, circa 1949.

Ronson products circa 1940.

Variety of popular Ronson Lighter/ Cigarette Case Combinations, circa 1942.

Ronson advertised the "World's Greatest Lighter" and manufactured pocket lighters, table lighters and cigarette/lighter combinations. In the 1940s, the Ronson "Mastercase" and "Supercase" made a big hit as the "perfect combination" of a handsome cigarette case and automatic lighter made of chromium plate. Other models incorporated tortoiseshell or enamel and chrome combinations. Ronson also offered cigarette cases made of "Dureum", a gold-colored alloy. A slightly different version of the Mastercase was called the "Tuxedo" case, also being a combination lighter and cigarette case. The "Tuxette" was the same case offered for women. In 1949, Ronson's famous double-duty "Penciliter" in rhodium plate retailed for $10.00. It was also available in 1/20 14K gold filled for $15.00. A mechanical pencil was positioned at one end and a lighter at the other "beautifully streamlined into one." For the lady, Ronson produced a compact/lighter combination, a compact/lighter/cigarette case combo, a perfume atomizer made in the shape of a lighter and lighters made in the shape of pocket watches. Other companies such as La Mode, Lin-Bren, Richard Hudnut, Evans, Dunhill, Marathon and Lampl manufactured combination compact and cigarette cases for women uniquely engineered and very desirable. Vanity case/cigarette case combinations were sometimes called "cigarette-vanettes."

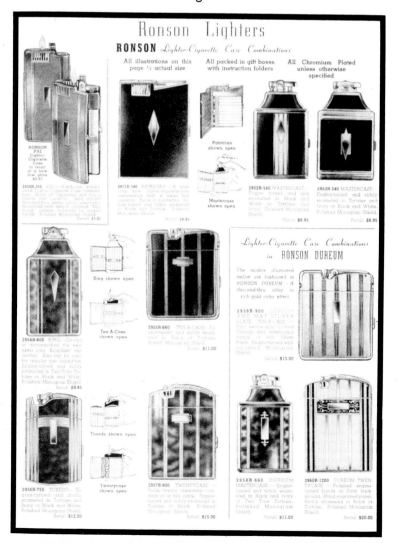

RONSON

Patented Other Pats Pdg
Trade Mark Registered

Perfu-Mist

Chromium Plate with Black, Red, Green, Blue, Tan, Brown or Grey Morocco Leathers.
List, each, $7.00

Chromium Plate with Genuine Snakeskin, Alligator or Ostrich.
List, each, $9.80

Green Gold Plate with Black, Red, Green, Blue, Tan, Brown or Grey Morocco Leathers.
List, each, $10.50

Green Gold Plate with Genuine Snakeskin, Alligator or Ostrich.
List, each, $13.30

Basket Weave Design
Barley Weave Design
Foxhead Design
Basket Weave Design

Chromium Plate, Engine Turned, Basket Weave, Barley Weave or Foxhead Designs.
List, each, $10.50

Green Gold, Engine Turned, Basket Weave, Barley Weave or Foxhead Designs.
List, each, $14.00

Chromium Plate with Black, Red, Green, Blue, Tan, Brown, or Grey Morocco Leathers.
List, each, $14.00

Green Gold Plate with Black, Red, Green, Blue, Tan, Brown or Grey Morocco Leathers.
List, each, $18.20

Also made in Sterling Silver.

Prices on application.

The World's Finest Perfume Spray

It works with magical simplicity

Chromium Plate, Engine Turned, Basket Weave, Barley Weave or Foxhead Designs.
List, each, $21.00

Green Gold Plate, Engine Turned, Basket Weave, Barley Weave or Foxhead Designs.
List, each, $25.20

Illustrations about

four-fifths actual size.

Ronson lighter-shaped Perfu-Mist atomizers popular in 1929, *The Keystone.*

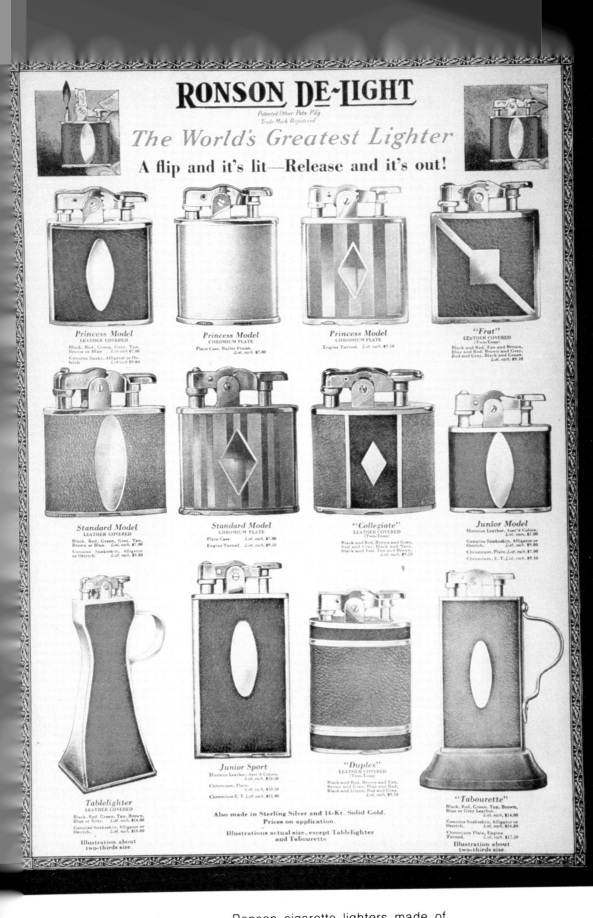

Ronson cigarette lighters made of chromium plate and genuine leather, *The Keystone*, 1929.

Ronson lighters offered for sale in 1942.

"Ronson Mastercase" combination cigarette case and lighter, marked "Ronson Art Metal Works, Inc., Newark, New Jersey, USA, Genuine chromium plate."

Two combination cigarette cases and lighters made of chromium plate by Ronson.

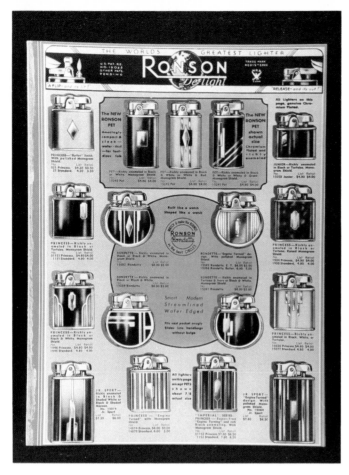

Modernistic Ronson Lighters, circa
1934-1935.

Ronson "Tuxedo" combination lighter
and cigarette case, circa 1934-1935.

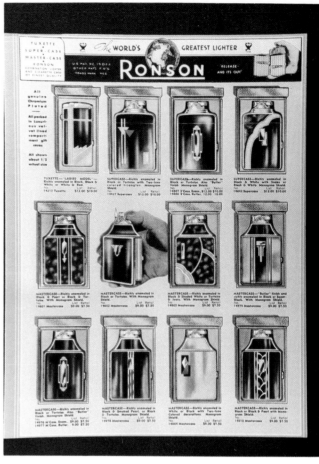

Ronson "Tuxette" combination lighter
and cigarette case designed for women
in 1934-1935.

Ronson Lighter and Cigarette Case
Sets for women.

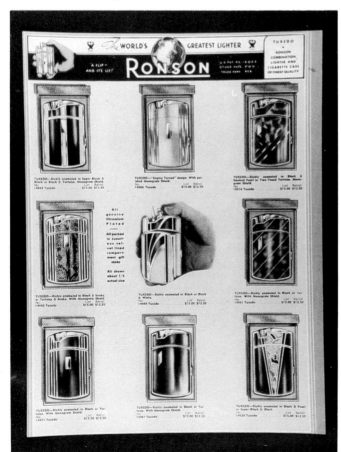

RONSON

Announces a Gigantic Advertising Campaign

Ronson DeLight

HEAVY Lighter advertising is behind the Ronson line this year—the most powerful campaign in the industry.

Full pages in the country's Sunday Rotogravure sections—a *Double page* in The Saturday Evening Post—a continuous drum-fire of dominating advertisements in Collier's, Cosmopolitan, American Magazine, Life, The New Yorker and The Saturday Evening Post.

This is a word to the wise. Be sure you have adequate stocks of THE WORLD'S GREATEST LIGHTER!

Ronson Perfu-Mist

This new Ronson product for women tops every Christmas list. It's the perfect pocket-size perfume spray—meets every woman's need in a modern way. Press, *presto*—perfume *when* she wants it, *as* she wants it.

To be powerfully advertised to insure your sales—dominating space in The Saturday Evening Post, Cosmopolitan, Good Housekeeping, True Story, Vogue and The New Yorker.

Order now—while your jobber's stock is complete.

ART METAL WORKS, Inc., Newark, N.J.

IN CANADA: DOMINION ART METAL WORKS, LTD., TORONTO, ONTARIO

Ronson DeLight and Perfu-Mist advertised in 1929.

Ronson "Penciliter" popular in 1949.

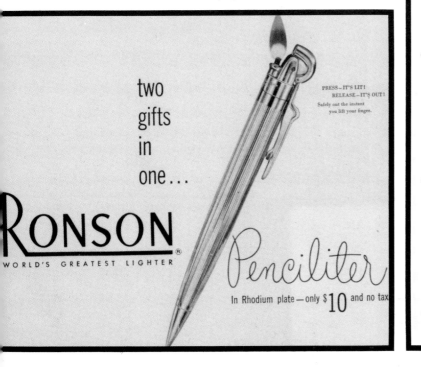

two gifts in one...

RONSON
WORLD'S GREATEST LIGHTER

Penciliter

PRESS—IT'S LIT!
RELEASE—IT'S OUT!
Safely out the instant you lift your finger.

In Rhodium plate — only $10 and no tax

RONSON
WORLD'S GREATEST LIGHTER

Personalized initials at no extra charge

Easy to refuel.. throw-away tank

LIGHTERS Built to Fine Jewelry Standards

PERSONALIZE the Ronson you select with initials at NO extra charge to you. When you write your Ronson order, specify the 3 initials you want engraved. Your Ronson will arrive personalized with 3 initials of your choice and it will cost you nothing additional.

[1] Graceful Ronson Windsor precision designed and gracefully contoured by Ronson craftsmen. Size 1⅝x1⅜-inch. Fashioned with chromium-plated fittings and a beautiful "gem-tone" Lumarith body. (Shipping weight 6 ounces.)
87 D R4595–Black Onyx finish. Postpaid..... $5.50
87 D R4596–Deep Ruby color finish. Postpaid..... $5.50

[2] Ronson Butane"Maximus" gives many more lights. With 2 throw-away Butanks. Uses no wick. Chrome-finish; 1¾-in. high. (Wt. 1 lb.)
87DR04573-Postpaid $12.50

[3] Bu-tank refill cartridges. Postpaid (Wt. 8 oz.)
87 D O4558.......... 2 for 75c

[4] Ronson Standard, a trim pocket lighter for men or women. 1⅝x1⅜-in. Works instantly. Press, it's lit—release, it's out. Chromium plate with silver-gray glow enamel finish. Handsomely boxed. A smart lighter to own or give. Postpaid. (Shipping weight 8 ounces.)
87 D R4581....... $6.95

[5] Ronson Whirlwind, 2-in-1 lighter with disappearing windshield. Large fuel capacity. 1⅞x2⅛-in. Satiny chromium-plated finish gives it distinction. Postpaid. (Wt. 8 oz.)
87 D R4577...... $9.60

[6] Ronson Standard Lighter with satin-effect all-chromium finish. Practical as well as beautiful, with the famous "press, it's lit; release, it's out" action. Size 1⅝x1⅜-inches. An ideal gift for both men and women. Postpaid. (Shipping weight 8 ounces.)
87 D R4574..... $7.70

[7] Ronson Princess Lighters. Petite, smart, compact—welcome accessories for any woman's handbag. Size 1⅝x1⅜-in. Boxed. Postpaid. (Wt. 8 oz.)
87D R4578-All chrome finish........... $7.70

Ronson lighters featured in the Sears catalogue in 1953.

Women's combination cigarette and compact cases popular in 1935.

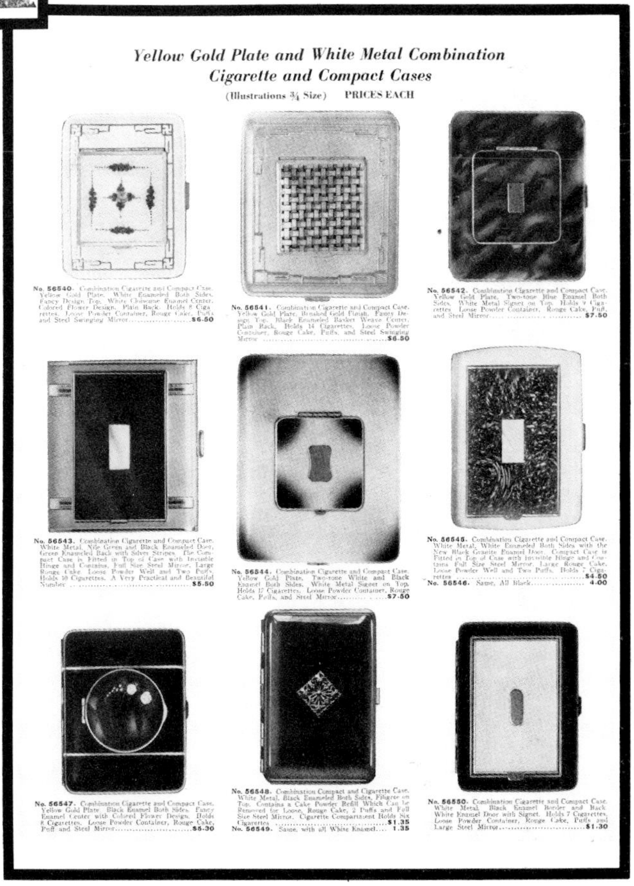

Yellow Gold Plate and White Metal Combination Cigarette and Compact Cases

(Illustrations ¾ Size)   PRICES EACH

No. 56840. Combination Cigarette and Compact Case. Yellow Gold Plate. White Enameled Both Sides. Fancy Design Top. White Cloisonne Enamel Center. Colored Flower Design. Plate Back. Holds 8 Cigarettes. Loose Powder Container, Rouge Cake and Steel Swinging Mirror........ $6.50

No. 56841. Combination Cigarette and Compact Case. Yellow Gold Plate. Beaded Gold Finish. Fancy Design Top. Plain Enameled Border Woven Center. Plain Back. Holds 16 Cigarettes. Loose Powder Container, Rouge Cake, Puffs, and Steel Swinging Mirror........ $6.50

No. 56842. Combination Cigarette and Compact Case. Yellow Gold Plate. Two-tone Blue Enamel Both Sides. White Metal Signet on Top. Holds 8 Cigarettes. Loose Powder Container, Rouge Cake, Puffs and Steel Mirror........ $7.50

No. 56843. Combination Cigarette and Compact Case. White Metal. Nile Green and Black Enameled Dove. Green Enameled Back with Silver Stripes. The Compact Case is Fitted in Top of Case with Separate Cover and Signet in Front Same as No. 56840. Holds 8 Cigarettes. Large Rouge Cake. Loose Powder Well and Two Puffs. A Very Practical and Beautiful Number........ $5.50

No. 56844. Combination Cigarette and Compact Case. Yellow Gold Plate. Two-tone White and Black Enamel Both Sides. White Metal Signet on Top. Holds 8 Cigarettes. Loose Powder Container, Rouge Cake, Puffs, and Steel Mirror........ $7.50

No. 56845. Combination Cigarette and Compact Case. White Metal. White Enameled Both Sides with the New Black Granite Enamel Inlay. Compact Case is Fitted in Top of Case with Invisible Hinge and Cover. Same as No. 56840. Holds 8 Cigarettes. Loose Powder Well and Two Puffs. Holds 12 Cigarettes........ $4.50
No. 56846. Same, All Black........ 4.00

No. 56847. Combination Cigarette and Compact Case. Yellow Gold Plate. Black Enameled Both Sides. Top Contains a Cake Powder Refill Which Can be Removed to Loose. Rouge Cake. 2 Puffs and Full Size Steel Mirror. Cigarette Compartment Holds Six Cigarettes........ $6.50
No. 56849. Same, with all White Enamel........ 1.35

No. 56850. Combination Compact and Cigarette Case. White Metal. Black Enameled Border and Black White Enamel Door with Signet. Holds 7 Cigarettes. Loose Powder Container, Rouge Cake, Puffs and Large Steel Mirror........ $1.30

Variety of imitation mother-of-pearl lighters with some hand engraving fashioned by Marhill.

Lighters and matching contact lens cases made of imitation mother-of-pearl decorated with hand painting, marked Essay, Japan, circa 1960s.

Zippo Windproof Lighters, circa 1947.

Zippo was famous for windproof lighters made of brush-finished or triple-plated chrome. The Regens Automatic "Stormliter" was advertised to light in any weather. It was manufactured in chrome or nickel. The A.S.R.(American Safety Razor Corporation) luxury lighter became popular because once lit, it stayed lit without holding. Every manufacturer had a gimmick which they used to promote their product.

Alfred Dunhill of London is a respected name in the manufacture of smoking accessories. Finely crafted genuine leather cigarette cases were designed in alligator leather as well as ostrich and pig skin; the former being made in Brazil and the latter made in U.S.Zone-Germany. Dunhill also used saddle lamb leather in red or tobacco brown for making cigarette cases designed to hold a full pack of cigarettes. These cases were designed with metal slide openings and zippered bottoms. Finely-crafted solid gold cigarette cases and lighters were also produced from this company and vintage examples are fetching high prices at recent auctions.

22522222222232222222222222222222222222222222222322

222

Novelty cigarette lighter made to look like a camera on a tripod, Photo-Lite Corp., Chicago, Illinois.

Three goldtone lighters embellished with colored glass stones and pearls arranged in floral designs, Made In Japan.

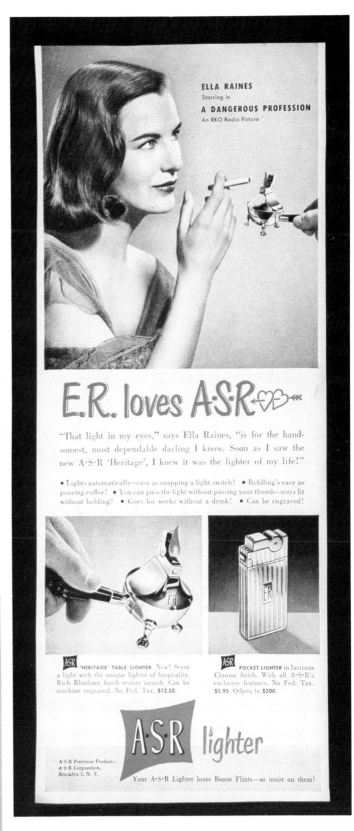

ELLA RAINES
Starring in
A DANGEROUS PROFESSION
An RKO Radio Picture

E.R. loves A·S·R

"That light in my eyes," says Ella Raines, "is for the handsomest, most dependable darling I know. Soon as I saw the new A·S·R 'Heritage', I knew it was the lighter of my life!"

• Lights automatically—easy as snapping a light switch! • Refilling's easy as pouring coffee! • You can pass the light without passing your thumb—*stays* lit without holding! • Goes for weeks without a drink! • Can be engraved!

'HERITAGE' TABLE LIGHTER. New! Serve a light with the unique lighter of hospitality. Rich Rhodium finish resists tarnish. Can be machine engraved. No Fed. Tax. $12.50.

POCKET LIGHTER in lustrous Chrome finish. With all A·S·R's exclusive features. No Fed. Tax. $5.95. Others to $200.

A·S·R lighter

A·S·R Precision Product—
A·S·R Corporation,
Brooklyn 1, N. Y.

Your A·S·R Lighter loves Boone Flints—so insist on them!

A.S.R. Lighters (American Safety Razor Corporation, makers of Gem Razors) advertised in 1949.

Seven jeweled cigarette lighters, marked Wiesner of Miami.

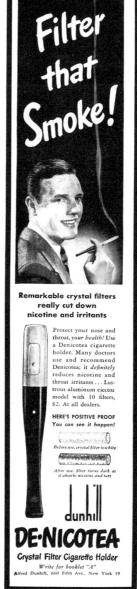

Filter that Smoke!

Remarkable crystal filters really cut down nicotine and irritants

Protect your nose and throat, *your health!* Use a Denicotea cigarette holder. Many doctors use and recommend Denicotea; it *definitely* reduces nicotine and throat irritants ... Lustrous aluminum ejector model with 10 filters, $2. At all dealers.

HERE'S POSITIVE PROOF You can see it happen!

Before use, crystal filter is white

After use, filter turns dark as it absorbs nicotine and tars

dunhill
DE·NICOTEA
Crystal Filter Cigarette Holder
Write for booklet "A"
Alfred Dunhill, 660 Fifth Ave., New York 19

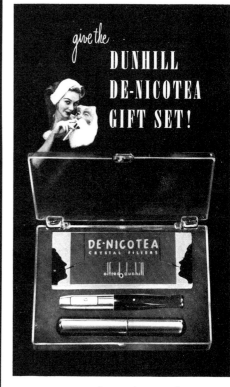

give the **DUNHILL DE·NICOTEA GIFT SET!**

for every cigarette smoker on your Christmas list

The gift that makes smoking safer, more pleasurable! It is really *four* gifts in one, for it contains:

• Our newest short Denicotea filter cigarette holder with gold-tone ejector.
• A holder for the holder—a matching gold-tone metal case to protect holder in pocket or purse.
• A supply of extra Denicotea crystal filters.
• All in a clear plastic package that makes a smart cigarette case, or box for table or desk.
  Dunhill Gift Set, $3.50 ... at stores everywhere.

dunhill

DE·NICOTEA CRYSTAL FILTER CIGARETTE HOLDER
FOR SMOKERS WHO THINK

Alfred Dunhill promoting crystal filters to reduce nicotine in 1953.

Although smoking was still fashionable when this ad was placed in *Life* in 1947, health concerns were really beginning to surface. Dunhill wanted to do something about it.

Six Propane lighters decorated with genuine and imitation leather, marked Brother-Lite

Genuine leather cigarette case, marked "Made in Germany—US Zone" and Bakelite cigarette holder by Alfred Dunhill.

Cigarette Case Combinations featured in the Hagn's Holiday Gift Flyer, circa 1934.

Genuine alligator cigarette case made in Brazil; Genuine snakeskin cigarette case by Alfred Dunhill.

Ritepoint cigarette lighters advertised in *Life*, circa 1949.

Leather accessories by C.F.Rumpp & Sons, Philadelphia, Pa., circa 1947.

Rumpps was another popular name associated with the manufacture of cigarette cases and other fashion accessories. In the 1950s, Rumpps manufactured cowhide cigarette cases and matching lighters in pink, blue, yellow, forest green and antique white-colored cowhide. Other accessories were made to coordinate with the smoking accessories. Eyeglass cases, compacts, pill boxes and wallets were also produced in genuine cowhide which was easy to keep clean with a damp cloth or a mild soap. The cigarette case was designed to hold one whole pack of cigarettes and opened from the top. These "Snapak" cases had an embossed gold circle located on one of the sides and when pushed in, the metal top would quickly unfold.

Rumpps genuine cowhide cigarette cases with spring tension lids designed to hold one full pack of cigarettes.

Gift sets

Gift sets became available for men and women containing a cigarette case with a matching lighter. More elaborate sets were offered for men containing a cigarette case, lighter, pocketknife, key case and wallet. Sets of all kinds were geared toward the man or woman who "took pleasure in smoking."

When smoking was glamorous, glamorous accessories accompanied this habit. Fine jewelers like Cartier, Fouquet, Templier and Tiffany rendered these accessories in solid gold, platinum and silver gilt, sometimes commissioned by the rich and famous. Recent auctions have shown us that celebrity-owned

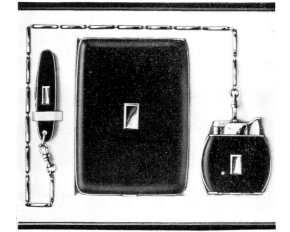

Men's Gift Sets consisting of cigarette case, pocket lighter, Waldemar chain and two-blade matching pocket knife, H.M.Manheim Company, circa 1933.

Cigarette cases and lighters offered from Sears, Roebuck & Company in 1938.

2-pc. DE LUXE GIFT SET. HALVORFOLD and 6-swivel hook Key Case. Ship O' Dreams design on back.
H-154 Steerhide.... $11.00

2-pc. DE LUXE GIFT SET. HALVORFOLD and 6-swivel hook Key Case.
H-153 Black Calf... $6.75
H-152 Brown Calf... $6.75

3-pc. DE LUXE GIFT SET, consisting of HALVOR-FOLD, 6-swivel hook Key Case and Cigarette Case. Each with good luck Ship O' Dreams design on back.
H-1480 Genuine Handlaced Steerhide.......... $13.00

DeLuxe Leather Gift Sets stylish in 1933.

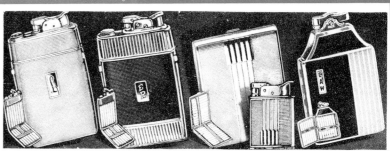

Handy Combination Cigarette Cases and Lighters

Specially Priced Evans Combination
Flip the lever, light your cigarette; release lever, flame is put out. White chromium plate or yellow gold color. Holds 14 cigarettes; size, 2½x4⅜ inches. Hand engraved initial. **Print initial.** Shipping weight, 13 ounces.
Chromium Plated.
4 K 5504......$1.79
Yellow Gold Finish
4 K 5505..... 2.89

Hand Engraved Initials
Initials for easy indentification and personal touch. On black enamel background. Yellow gold color metal or white chromium plated. Holds 14 cigarettes. 2½x4⅜ in. Two initials hand engraved. **Print initials.** Shipping weight, 13 oz.
Gold Color
4 K 5612......$3.69
Chromium Plated
4 K 5613...... 2.69

Matching Lighter and Case
The perfect gift for men or women. Charming yellow gold color metal. Attractive modern design case is 4x3 in., holds 20 cigarettes—a full package! Lighter to match.
4K5614—Complete Set. Shipping weight, 14 ounces... **$1.98**
4K5615—Case only.
Shpg. wt., 8 oz...98c
4K5616—Lighter only.
Shpg. wt., 5 oz..$1.19

"Ronson's Mastercase"
Our finest combination. White chromium plate or Durium, gleaming yellow gold color metal with harmonizing black enamel. Holds 14 cigarettes. 2½x4¼ in. Any initials hand engraved. **Print initials. Postpaid.**
Chromium Plated
4 K 5517......$7.95
4 K 5518—Durium (design differs slightly from picture)....$10.00

DISTINCTIVE LIGHTERS FOR DISTINCTIVE PERSONS

Dependable Evans Automatic
Every snap a light, with this Evans lighter that's famous for its dependable action! Attractively designed. A perfect gift for the smoker. Convenient size, about 1⅞ x 1⅜ in. Any initial hand engraved. **Print initial wanted.** Shipping weight, 5 ounces.
Chromium Plated.
4 K 5546......98c
Yellow Gold Color.
4 K 5547......$1.79

Leather Covered Ronson
$5.00 used to be the price of this handsome black leather-covered chromium plated Ronson lighter. This lighter will give you a quick flame every time. Raised shield with any initials hand engraved. Size, 1⅞ x 1⅝ inches.**Print initials wanted.** Shipping weight, 5 ounces.
4 K 5511......$2.98

Swanky Ronson Standard
Beautiful engraved design sets off the gleaming white of this chromium plated lighter. Fast, trusty action for cigarette, cigar, or pipe. A Ronson lighter is known to be one of the best. Handy for man's pocket or woman's purse; size, about 2x 1½ in. Any initials hand engraved—a perfect gift. **Print initials. Postpaid.**
4 K 5548...$3.75

Ronson Pencil Lighter
A useful gift for the man smoker—one that he'll use every day, both as a lighter and as a pencil. The automatic Ronson lighter fits snugly into the top of the attractive propel-repel-expel pencil. Richly engraved chromium plate with green pearl color pencil barrel. Has safety pocket clip to prevent loss. Length over all, about 5½ in. Has proven a most popular gift. In gift box. **Postpaid.**
4 K 5507......$4.50

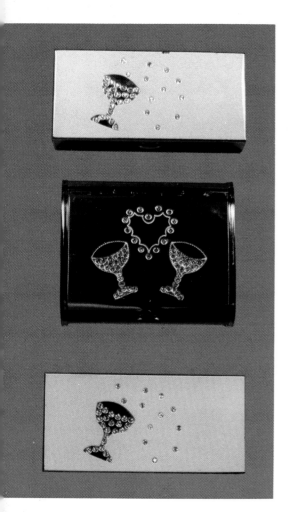

Three cigarette cases decorated with rhinestone champagne glasses.

accessories are bringing exorbitant prices. For example, a sterling silver cigarette case once belonging to Rita Hayworth sold for over $5000. Another sterling cigarette case given by Humphrey Bogart to his wife Mayo in 1938, sold for over $6000. Ironically, a solid gold and black enameled cigarette case with a diamond monogram, made by Cartier in 1930, was auctioned a few years ago as part of the Andy Warhol collection. This case, with all of its Art Deco splendor, sold for a little over $4000. The value of an item depends not only on its material but also on a host of other factors including rarity of a design, the complexity upon which the design was rendered, if it is hand made, its age, condition, or whether it was manufactured, designed, signed or owned by someone famous.

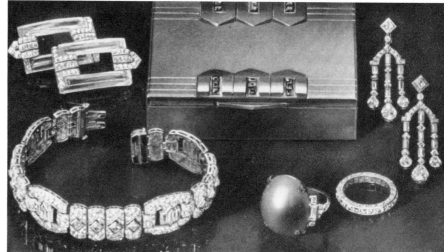

DIAMOND AND CRYSTAL CLIPS $765 THE PAIR, DIAMOND BRACELET $3550, JADE AN[D] DIAMOND RING $1250, DIAMOND BAND RING $470, DIAMOND EARRINGS $4200 TH[E] PAIR; GOLD CIGARETTE CASE ORNAMENTED WITH SQUARE-CUT SAPPHIRES $43[...]

Gold and sapphire cigarette case by Tiffany & Company advertised in *Harper's Bazaar*, April, 1936.

Silver cigarette case by Udall and Ballou advertised in *Harper's Bazaar*, April, 1936.

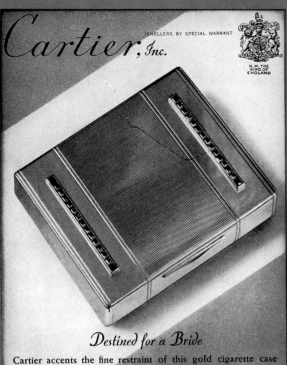

Gold and sapphire cigarette case by Cartier advertised in *Harper's Bazaar*, May, 1938.

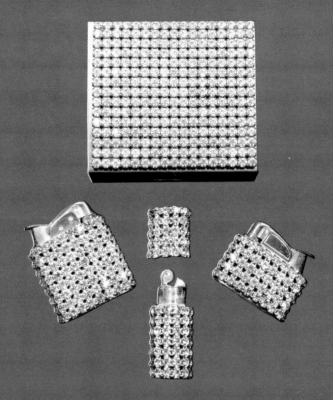

Rhinestone studded cigarette case and three rhinestone cigarette lighters, Trickettes by Wiesner of Miami.

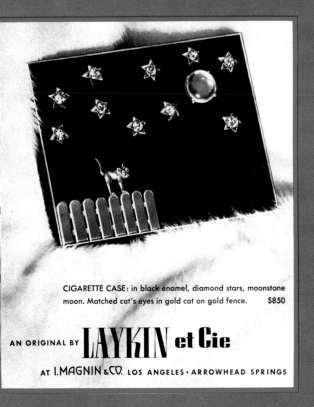

Jeweled cigarette case by Laykin et Cie, *Harper's Bazaar*, January, 1940.

Jeweled cigarette case made of imitation pearls and rhinestones.

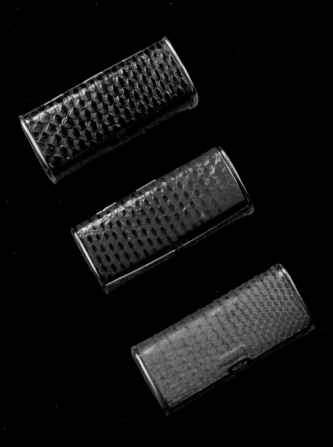

Three dyed snakeskin cigarette cases.

Three snakeskin cigarette cases.

Three jeweled cigarette cases.

White enameled cigarette case with raised red enameled beads set with rhinestones; Pink enameled cigarette case set with rhinestones.

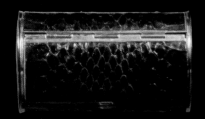

Pink Lucite slimline cigarette case.

Compact and cigarette case combination made of dyed leather, marked Lin-Bren.

Two pearl-topped slim style cigarette cases made by Wiesner of Miami.

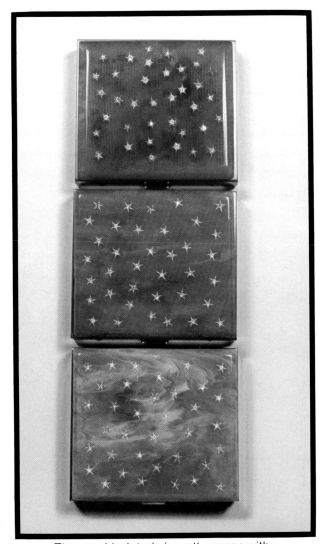

Three gold-plated cigarette cases with Bakelite tops enriched with rhinestones.

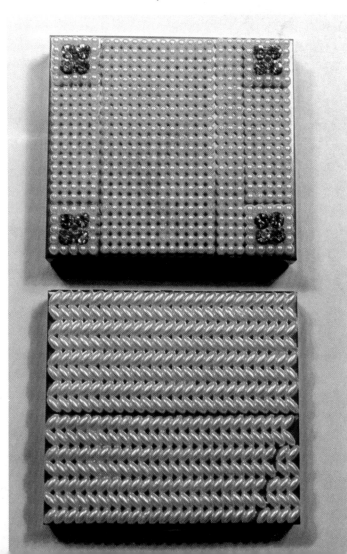

Cigarette case and retractable purse comb encrusted with clear and amethyst-colored glass stones.

Speckled Lucite cigarette cases made by Curry Arts; Large Lucite cigarette lighter by Supreme; Small Lucite cigarette lighter by Evans.

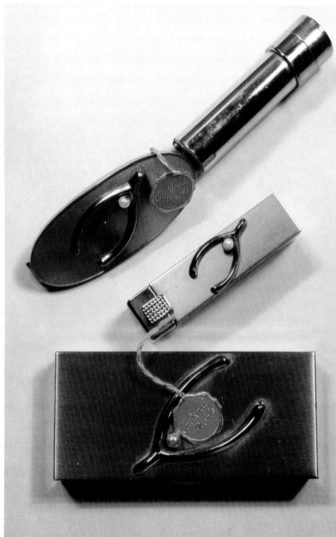

Matched set consisting of cigarette case and two lipvues made of brushed goldtone metal ornamented with a wishbone set with a cultured pearl, marked K & K.

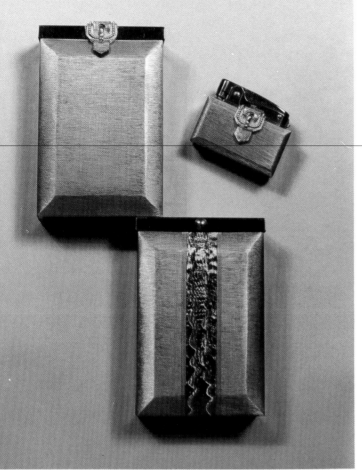

Traditional style brushed gold and hand engraved cigarette cases, marked Marhill; Matching cigarette lighter, marked "Pigeon Automatic Super Lighter, Japan."

Enameled, hand painted and lacquered cigarette case and matching lighter made in Japan.

Two goldtone armor mesh cigarette cases with zippered closures made by Duramesh, Fifth Avenue.

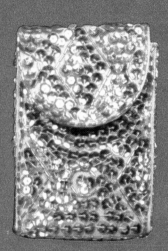

Silver and gold sequined cigarette cases by La Regalé.

Cigarette case made of white seed beads and pearlized sequins, marked Hand Made in Hong Kong.

Goldtone and silvertone mesh cigarette cases with original box which reads: "Mesh-Mates made of Oromesh by Whiting and Davis".

Two imitation mother-of-pearl cigarette cases.

Imitation tortoiseshell cigarette case designed to hold full pack of cigarettes.

Three imitation mother-of-pearl cigarette cases designed to hold full pack of cigarettes.

Gold mesh lipstick tube and musical cigarette lighter by Pacton, Made in Japan.

Two pink confetti Lucite cigarette cases.

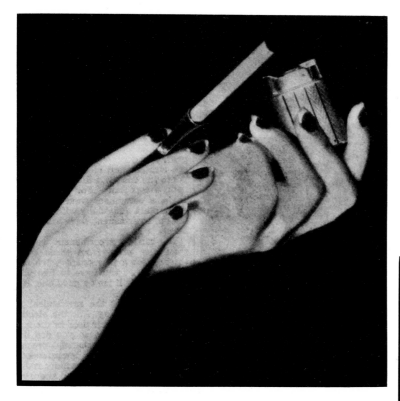

Black beadlite enameled mesh cigarette lighter and red, white and blue armor mesh cigarette lighter by Whiting and Davis.

Two imitation mother-of-pearl cigarette cases, one decorated with multi-colored glass stones.

Bibliography

Books

Angeloglou, Maggie. *A History of Make-up*. London: Studio Vista Ltd., 1970.

Cunnington, C. Willett and Phillis Cunnington. *Handbook of English Costume in the Nineteenth Century*. Great Britian: Dufour Editions, 1959.

Gerson, Roselyn. *Ladies' Compacts of the Nineteenth and Twentieth Centuries*. Radnor, Pennsylvania: Wallace-Homestead Book Co., 1989.

Goldring, William. *The Pipe Book*. New York: Drake Publishers, Inc., 1973.

Gunn, Fenja, *The Artificial Face: A History of Cosmetics*. New York: Hippocrene Books Inc., 1973.

Meyer, Carolyn. *Being Beautiful, The Story of Cosmetics From Ancient Art to Modern Science*. New York: William Morrow and Company, 1977.

Shuker, Nancy. *Elizabeth Arden*. Englewood Cliffs, New Jersey: Silver Burdett Press, 1989.

Catalogs

Aldens, Chicago, Illinois, Spring and Summer, 1959.

Benj. Allen & Co. Inc., Chicago, Illinois, 1935.

Bennett Blue Book, Chicago and New York, 1966.

BHA Illustrated Catalogue, Schwenksville, Pennsylvania, 1895.

Bloomingdale's Illustrated 1886 Catalog, Dover Reprint, 1988.

Boston Store, Chicago, Illinois, Fall and Winter, 1910/1911.

Butler Brothers Dry Goods, January, 1937.

Carson Pirie Scott & Co., Chicago, Illinois, 1942.

Chicago Mail Order Company, Chicago, Illinois, 1911/1912.

Christie's East Auction Catalogs, New York, 1987 and 1988.

Fort Dearborn Watch & Clock Company, Chicago, 1923/1924.

Hagn's Holiday Gift Flyer, 1934.

H.M. Manheim & Company, Catalogue # 72, New York, 1933.

Jason Weiler & Sons, Boston, Mass., 1927.

John V. Farwell Company, Chicago, 1920/1921.

John Wanamaker Store & Home Catalogue, Philadelphia, 1913.

Lee-Robert Company, Chicago, Illinois, 1950/1951.

Lyon Brothers Catalog #258, Chicago, 1899-1900.

M. Gerber Wholesale Company, Philadelphia, 1899/1900.

Montgomery Ward & Company, Chicago, 1895, 1922, 1937/1938 and 1953.

National Bellas Hess Company, New York & Kansas City, 1928.

National Cloak and Suit Company, 1925.

Sears, Roebuck & Company, Chicago & Philadelphia, 1900, 1902, 1909, 1927, 1930, 1937, 1938, 1939, 1942, 1943-44, 1946-47, 1949, 1951, 1953, 1955 and 1963.

Skinner Auction Catalogs, Boston, Mass., 1988.

Sotheby's Auction Catalogs (Jewelry), New York, 1988, 1989, 1990 and 1991.

Spiegel, Spring and Summer, 1948 and 1951.

Magazines

Best Songs (September, 1946).
Delineator (1884, 1902, 1928, 1932, 1933 and 1935).
Designer (1905, 1912 and 1923).
Harper's Bazaar (1899, 1918, 1936, 1937, 1938, 1939, 1940 and 1957).
Keystone (September 1929).
Ladies' Home Journal (1891, 1893, 1897, 1903, 1909, 1912, 1928, 1933, 1944 and 1952).
Life (1940, 1947, 1948, 1949, 1951 and 1953).
McCall's (1908, 1910, 1911, 1912, 1916, 1917, 1932, 1936, 1938, 1939, 1943 and 1949).
Modern Pricilla (March, 1916).
Peoples' Home Journal (November, 1911).
Pictorial Review (1922, 1935 and 1936).
Popular Songs (May, 1935).
Ridley's Fashion Magazine (1882 and 1883).
Seventeen (1947, 1948 and 1958).
Song Hits Magazine (March, 1943).
To-Day's Magazine (Feb.15, 1912).
Woman's Home Companion (1953 and 1955).
Vogue (1917, 1918, 1919, 1936, 1937, 1938, 1939, 1947 and 1960).

Newspapers

Evening Public Ledger, Philadelphia, June, October and December, 1929 and 1930.
Happy Hours, 1913.
Philadelphia Inquirer, June, October and December, 1929 and 1930.

Values Guide

Values vary immensely according to an article's condition, location of the market, parts of the country, and overall quality of design. While one must make their own decisions, we can offer a guide. Compacts in original advertisements have not been valued.

SS - Sterling Silver
GS - German Silver

NS - Nickel Silver
SP - Silver Plate
M-o-P - Mother-of-Pearl

Chapter I		U.S. ($)	p-36.	Goldtone compact	80-100
				Art Deco vanity cases	100-135
p-17.	Powder refills	20-40		Necessaire	1200-1500
	Rouge refills	20-40	p-37.	Vanity cases	75-100
	Powder containers	35-50		Elgin American	110-145
	Rouge containers	35-50	p-38.	Celluloid mirrors	25-50
				Celluloid compacts	50-75
				Chrome compact	50-75
				Octagonal vanity	40-60
Chapter II				Dorothy Gray vanity	50-75
				Flapjack compact	65-85
p-20.	Vanity case	350-500	p-39.	Brass compacts	50-100
p-21.	Vanity case	80-150	p-40.	Austrian compacts	150-200
p-22.	SS vanity case	175-225	p-41.	Beaded compacts	175-250
	Brass vanity case	120-150		Brass compact	100-150
	GS vanity case	130-165		Plastic compact	40-60
p-23.	SS vanity purse	200-250	p-42.	Hand engraved compact	125-175
	Embossed vanity case	135-175	p-43.	Watchcase compact	150-200
p-24.	Engraved vanity case	145-195		Coty compacts	50-100
p-26.	Vanity case	125-175		Petitpoint compact	75-125
p-27.	Ornate vanity cases	200-400	p-44.	Watchcase compacts	125-200
	Round case	135-185		Floral transfer	55-80
	Chromium cases	100-150		Celluloid compact	45-75
p-28.	14K gold case	1800-2000		Black enameled compact	50-75
	Mirror vanity case	60-85		Square scenic	45-65
	Star-shaped vanity	100-150		Two rectangular compacts	35-60
p-30.	Plated vanity cases	115-165	p-45.	Large compact	80-115
	Oval vanity case	130-180		Three enameled compacts	75-175
p-31.	Finger ring vanity	80-135		Butterfly wing	55-80
	Terri vanity cases	100-145		Engraved compact	100-150
	Enameled triple vanity	175-250	p-46.	Flapjack compact	80-115
p-32.	Finger ring vanities	150-300		Figural transfer	50-75
p-33.	Oval vanity case	85-115		Jeweled compacts	45-75
	Evans vanity case	85-125	p-47-50.	Lucite lipvues	25-65
	Cloisonné compact	135-175		Lucite perfume vials	35-65
p-34.	Octagonal vanity case	150-200		Lucite billfolds	50-85
	Pink enameled case	75-95		Lucite purse combs	25-45
	Chromium-plated case	110-175		Lucite compacts (various	
	Double vanity	50-75		shapes and sizes)	50-100
	Atarmist	75-125		Lucite lipstick cases	25-50
p-35.	Minaudière	600-850			

Index